The Untapped World Of SEXUAL Intimacy

Foreword By
Lerato Charlotte Letsoso

The Untapped World Of SEXUAL Intimacy

Disego Nkoana

All Rights Reserved

No part of this publication may be reproduced, stored in a retrieval system, or transmitted in any form or by any means – electronic, mechanical, photocopying, recording or otherwise – without written permission from the publisher, except per the provisions of the Copyright Act, 98 of 1978.

Copyright © Disego Nkoana 2024

The Untapped World Of Sexual Intimacy

ISBN: 978-0-7961-7010-1

Published by:

Graceworx Publishers, Pretoria

50 Modumbla Cul De Sac, Lotus Gardens, Pretoria West

0818398946 | disegonkoana@gmail.com

Content Editing, Layout & Cover Design:

Graceworx Publishers

Published In The Republic Of South Africa

Other Books:

Social Media:
Disego Nkoana

Whatsapp: +27 81 839 8946
Email: disegonkoana@gmail.com

Other Books By Disego Nkoana

The Paradigms Of Love
2018
Graceworx Publishers

Mended Heart
2021
Graceworx Publishers

Dedications

While in the process of writing this book, my mom, Maria Motsatsi Nkoana, left us to be reunited with her late husband, Mashole Gideon Nkoana. I dedicate this book to her memory. To my dad, who passed on in 2003, you are the inspiration behind my writing. I know you were writing a book which you would have loved to have been published but you could not. Thank you for igniting a flame within me.

To my siblings, Mpho, Tshepiso, Katlego, Khomotso, and my niece, Kamogelo, this book goes to you too. I love you and thank you for believing in me so much.

To all my friends who have since become family, those I would text time and again asking some deeply personal questions and you did not hold back, I may not mention you all, but Nare, Unathi, Olga, Louisah, Mpho, and all of you who never seize to give me your forever present support, I appreciate you and I dedicate this one to you.

Lastly, to you who hand-picked this book and ready to turn to the left every page, you are the star of the show. Kudus to you

Foreword

I know the first thing that comes to mind when we talk about physical intimacy is sex. And although that is very much a type of physical intimacy, it is just one part, there are many other forms of physical intimacy.

Physical intimacy is between bodies, emotional intimacy between hearts, intellectual intimacy between minds and spiritual intimacy is what occurs when a soul touches another soul. Physical intimacy is essentially about touch and closeness between bodies. In a romantic relationship, it might include holding hands, cuddling, kissing, and sex.

Intimacy is a beautiful thing, however for some reason not many people are comfortable in displaying it. Whether publicly or privately, intimacy remains a challenge for many individuals especially those from conventional backgrounds. However, in his book " The untapped world of sexual intimacy." Disego Nkoana pans his lens on the specific area of sexual intimacy in a bohemian way.

Taking into account Disego's experience as a preacher of the word of God, it is particularly refreshing that he is not shy to tackle topics that are usually controversial within the religious community. I should think that his background as a relationships counsellor and coach has had profound impact in his posture regarding romantic relationships in general and in extension has influenced his writing in this particular offering.

In this book, I enjoy the education that comes with an invitation to break the stigma surrounding sex especially in the Christian community. Through these petite nine chapters, Disego successfully takes us through an enlightening funnel of sexual intimacy enough to not only ventilate but also to enable any individual to take on a much sober and objective approach when it comes to their sexual discipline. Furthermore, I feel "The untapped world of sexual intimacy" would make an ideal material for new couples or those who struggle to open up in the area of sex.

Lerato Charlotte Letsoso
Intimacy Coach, Speaker and award-winning author

TABLE OF CONTENTS

Introduction		*1*
Chapter 1	The Significance Of Sexual Intimacy	*6*
Chapter 2	Debunking The Myths And Misconceptions	*16*
Chapter 3	Common Challenges In Sexual Intimacy	*50*
Chapter 4	The Harsh Realities Of Sexual Intimacy	*98*
Chapter 5	Redefining Sexual Intimacy	*114*
Chapter 6	The essence Of Sexual Intimacy	*130*
Chapter 7	Exploring Male & Female Psychology In Sexual Intimacy	*150*
Chapter 8	Exploring Male & Female Physiology In Sexual Intimacy	*168*
Chapter 9	The Art Of Sexual Intimacy	*194*

Dear Reader,

In a world saturated with information, I offer you a beacon of enlightenment—a gift of consolation and guidance found within the pages of this book. At a time when relationships are strained and long-term commitments dissolve due to bedroom dissatisfaction, I extend to you a lifeline—a source of understanding and illumination in the realm of sexuality.

This book is tailored to meet you wherever you are on your journey. Whether you're married and seeking a deeper connection, engaged and preparing for the road ahead, or single and exploring your own sexuality, its pages are designed to empower and enlighten.

Thank you for hand-picking this book, and I trust this letter finds you well, navigating the complexities of intimacy with resilience and hope. May this book serve as a compass, guiding you toward fulfillment and contentment in your relationships.

Warm regards,

Disego

INTRODUCTION

There's a natural curiosity about something deeply human—sexual intimacy. Right from when we're little, we start wondering about it. But here's the tricky part: there's no special school to teach us about it. Most of us end up learning from the streets, the internet, or odd places where information gets mixed up. Some folks even turn sex into something religious, and traditional views can steer us away from what it really is.

Sadly, many people grow up not knowing much about sex. It's like a secret club that no one talks about. Parents find it hard to have "the talk," and kids feel too embarrassed to ask. So, they end up learning from unreliable sources, which can be confusing.

Let me share a story about my younger brother and niece when they were just 5 and 6 years old. I had to babysit them for a day, and these curious little explorers decided to investigate something under a bed. I found my brother lying on top of my niece, they were clearly clueless on what they were doing but they made me realise that as humans, our curiosity spans from early childhood. It turned out, they got the idea from other kids at pre-school. But here's the point: from a very young age, we humans are super curious, especially about intimacy.

How we learn about intimacy early on, whether someone talks to us or we see something, can stick with us for a long time. Some people have tough experiences, like abuse, that shape how they see intimacy. This can affect them for their whole lives, unless they get some help.

Now, let's talk about why this all matters. Sexual intimacy is like the secret sauce that helps relationships stay healthy. It's the special ingredient that adds closeness, trust, and happiness. Think of it as the glue that keeps partners connected. When two people share intimate moments, it's not just about the physical act—it's about building a strong bond that goes

The Significance Of Sexual Intimacy In Relationships

beyond words. Many couples are so focused on making time for the physical act so much that they forget to make time just to be with each other. An intimacy time together is much more valuable than the physical act and if we prioritize the physical more than we prioritize each other, the sex will eventually lose its value and we will no longer enjoy it.

In the chapters ahead, we'll explore why it's a key ingredient and how it can transform relationships for the better. Stick around as we uncover the layers and discover the real magic of intimacy that fosters healthy, thriving connections.

The Goal of This Book

Now, let's talk about why this book exists. The goal here is to debunk the myths and misconceptions surrounding sexual intimacy. It's like shining a light on a path that's often shrouded in darkness. I want to take you on a journey—a journey into a whole new world that many people have never known before.

My aim is to open your eyes to the profound depth of sexual intimacy. I believe that understanding this depth can help reshape your world of sexual pleasure and connection. I don't want to dictate to you how to view sexual intimacy, instead, I want to share thoughts with you, which I believe could make a positive difference in your life.

Perhaps, we will learn to be faithful to our partners and have relationships that are not just committed but are also sexually fulfilling. Stick with me as we navigate through the pages, uncovering layers, and discovering the real magic of intimacy—a magic that has the potential to transform not just our relationships but our entire approach to closeness and pleasure.

Sex Beyond the Physical

Sex is a profound journey that goes far beyond just vaginal penetration or genital stimulation. It's an intricate dance that extends beyond the confines of the bedroom, reaching into the core of how we communicate and treat each other. The true essence of a pleasurable physical experience lies in how we make each other feel long before we even think about getting naked.

In this book, we will explore dimensions of intimacy that precede the physical. It's about understanding that the groundwork for a fulfilling physical connection is laid through emotional closeness, trust, and effective communication. We'll delve into the importance of emotional intimacy, the nuances of building trust, and the art of communication that forms the foundation of a strong, healthy relationship. Only after navigating through these dimensions will we embark on the exploration of the physical aspect of sexual intimacy, recognizing its connection to the web of emotions, trust, and communication. Stick around as we unravel the layers of intimacy, uncovering its true depth and beauty.

Embarking on a Journey of Discovery

As we embark on this exploration, consider this book not just as a guide but as a companion. Together, we'll navigate through the complexities of sexual intimacy, acknowledging that it's a journey encompassing emotional, psychological, and physical facets. Beyond the misconceptions, myths, societal pressures, and personal inhibitions, we'll delve into a world where intimacy is not confined to societal norms but is a unique expression of connection and pleasure tailored for each individual and partnership.

Throughout these pages, expect insights, reflections, and practical advice that extend beyond conventional wisdom. This is not a prescriptive manual but an invitation to reflect, question, and redefine your perceptions of sexual intimacy. It's an acknowledgment that each person's journey is distinct, and the beauty of intimacy lies in its diversity.

So, whether you're exploring intimacy for the first time, navigating a long-term partnership, or rediscovering your connection with a loved one, let's embark on this journey together—a journey that transcends the physical and embraces the profound chemistry of human connection.

Chapter One

The Significance of Sexual Intimacy in Relationships

"The pursuit of physical pleasure without a sincere desire for emotional connection can result in emotional emptiness, loneliness, and a pattern of unsatisfying relationships."

The Significance Of Sexual Intimacy In Relationships

The significance of sexual intimacy in relationships lies in its ability to create a deep and fulfilling connection between partners, often regarded as the glue that binds them together. When individuals experience sexual frustration within a relationship, it's frequently a symptom of underlying issues or dissatisfaction rather than solely a result of physical intimacy.

It's intriguing how two individuals who embark on their relationship journey with happiness may eventually confront sexual frustration. This shift prompts questions about what changed along the way and what factors contributed to this development. Sustaining a consistently satisfying sexual relationship requires ongoing effort and dedication to keep the spark alive. However, in the course of a long-term relationship, a formidable adversary inevitably emerges: familiarity.

As a relationship coach, I often remind my clients that a lifetime is a very long time to spend with one person. It's essential to grasp the challenges that comes naturally with committing to a long-term partnership. Spending ample time with someone inevitably leads to familiarity, which can diminish the allure of absence making the heart grow fonder. The once-sexy voice that once stirred desire may become boring, and familiarity may obscure the qualities that initially attracted partners to each other, leading to a sense of fading love—a slow poison corroding the relationship.

Every relationship, regardless of its strength, faces trials over time that test its resilience and threaten its stability. As a coach, I've conversed with numerous couples still enjoying the honeymoon phase, encouraging them to brace themselves for potential challenges. Mostly, new couples are hesitant to contemplate the possibility of facing serious challenges in the relationship. Yet, reality is that relationships are complex, and as partners grow closer, they unearth both endearing and challenging aspects of each other.

Despite efforts to maintain perfection, no relationship is rainproof to human complexities and challenges. Navigating intimacy and emotional connection inevitably entails encountering rough patches. Acknowledging this reality isn't conceding defeat but rather recognizing the complexities of human relationships. Understanding this empowers couples to approach their union with resilience and adaptability, creating open communication, mutual understanding, and courage to confront discomfort.

Like an uninvited guest, familiarity infiltrates relationships subtly, and just like death, familiarity is inevitable. As the honeymoon phase fades, partners become entwined in routine, and the once-charming quirks become a commonplace. This transition can be confusing for couples accustomed to the excitement of new love. However, familiarity isn't inherently negative; it offers comfort and security, guiding partners through life's highs and lows.

Navigating this phase necessitates patience, understanding, and a willingness to embrace change. Relationships evolve, and embracing familiarity as part of this evolution builds resilience and enduring connection. Proactively addressing familiarity involves commitment to growth, both individually and as a couple, through shared experiences and personal development.

Sexual intimacy serves as a cornerstone in countering familiarity, offering a vibrant connection that transcends physical pleasure. Intentionality in relationships emphasizes purposeful engagement and mutual affirmation. Addressing familiarity, consistency, and intention emphasises the importance of nurturing the relationship's flame through ongoing dialogue and understanding. In this context, familiarity becomes a navigable force, enriching the connection and enabling growth over time.

The Significance Of Sexual Intimacy In Relationships

The Role of Sexual Intimacy in Deepening Emotional Connection

Sexual intimacy plays a profound role in constructing and strengthening the emotional connections between partners. In the complexities of relationships, these emotional bonds serve as the very foundation on which the dynamics of a healthy and thriving connection rely. Without a robust emotional connection, a relationship faces the risk of stagnation, and the absence of this vital link may turn the partnership into an emotional battleground.

My experience as a relationship coach has shown the widespread issue of relationships lacking essential emotional connections. In such instances, unmet emotions can manifest like a volcano, ready to erupt and potentially consume individuals from within; ultimately consuming the relationship. The absence of emotional connection creates fertile ground for frustration, laying the groundwork for conflicts that can undermine the very fabric of the relationship.

It is crucial to discern between emotional connection and one-sided emotional attachments. The latter occurs when one person becomes emotionally dependent while the other remains emotionally distant. This imbalanced attachment often results in a continuous cycle of rejection for the emotionally invested individual, leading to heartbreak and an enduring void that proves challenging to mend. Making this crucial distinction is paramount for creating healthy emotional connections and ensuring that both partners contribute emotionally in a relationship.

Emotional connection, on the other hand, is a subtle dance, requiring a delicate balance of vulnerability, empathy, and genuine understanding. It goes beyond mere verbal expressions of love; it involves an intuitive exchange of emotions that creates a shared emotional landscape for both partners. This connection builds a safe space where individuals feel seen, heard, and accepted in their entirety. It goes beyond the surface, delving into the core of each person's emotional world, creating a profound sense of intimacy that forms the backbone of a lasting relationship.

Moreover, emotional connection serves as a reservoir of strength during challenging times. When couples navigate life's inevitable ups and downs, a strong emotional bond becomes a source of support and reassurance. It acts as a buffer against external stressors, providing a foundation upon which both partners can lean. In moments of joy, it amplifies the celebration, and in times of sorrow, it offers solace. This shared emotional reservoir becomes a source of strength and endurance for the relationship, standing resilient against the tests of time.

Sexual intimacy plays a special role in making the emotional bond between partners stronger. It's like a unique language of love and desire that goes beyond words. When we're physically close, sharing our vulnerabilities and exploring together, it adds a deep layer to our emotional connection.

Being intimate physically brings partners even closer emotionally. Trust grows, and a sense of closeness extends beyond just the physical aspect. This shared trust becomes a link connecting the emotional and physical parts of the relationship.

Additionally, the good feelings that come from being intimate, like the release of happy hormones, contribute to an overall sense of happiness and well-being. This positive impact often continues in other parts of the relationship, creating a happy and connected atmosphere.

In simple terms, sexual intimacy is like a unique way of expressing emotions that makes the bond between partners stronger. It shows that there's trust and openness in the relationship, helping couples navigate their emotions together. The combination of physical and emotional closeness builds a strong and lasting connection between two people.

Sexual Intimacy and Physical Pleasure

Beyond emotional aspects, sexual intimacy provides a source of physical pleasure and satisfaction. The physical dimension of sexual intimacy

The Significance Of Sexual Intimacy In Relationships

contributes to the overall well-being of individuals, promoting a healthy balance between the emotional and physical aspects of the relationship.

The physical pleasure derived from sexual intimacy is a cornerstone of its significance in relationships. It goes beyond mere satisfaction; it is a unique expression of love and desire that contributes to the overall well-being of individuals. In the realm of physical pleasure, partners discover a shared language that goes beyond verbal communication, allowing them to connect on a primal level that words often fail to reach.

This physical dimension of intimacy promotes a holistic approach to well-being. The release of endorphins and the surge of positive hormones during sexual activities not only enhance mood but also contribute to stress relief. The physical closeness shared between partners becomes a sanctuary, providing a momentary escape from the pressures of everyday life. This intimate connection serves as a vital component in maintaining a healthy balance between the emotional and physical aspects of a relationship.

Moreover, the physical pleasure derived from sexual intimacy is a dynamic force that extends far beyond the bedroom. It has a ripple effect on the overall quality of the relationship, influencing how partners perceive and interact with each other in various aspects of their lives. The satisfaction gained from these shared moments of physical intimacy contributes to a positive feedback loop, reinforcing the emotional connection and creating a sense of mutual satisfaction.

In essence, the physical pleasure found in sexual intimacy is not only a momentary source of joy but a fundamental element that promotes overall well-being. It acts as a glue that binds partners together, creating a harmonious balance between the emotional depth of their connection and the physical joy derived from their intimate moments. As partners continue to explore and cherish these physical expressions of love, they cultivate a lasting source of satisfaction that enriches the depth of their relationship.

But while sexual intimacy is a beautiful and bonding experience, there exists a phenomenon where individuals may prioritize the pursuit of physical pleasure without a genuine desire for emotional connection. In contemporary culture, casual or purely physical relationships have become more prevalent, where the emphasis is on momentary satisfaction rather than the establishment of a deep emotional bond.

This pursuit of physical pleasure devoid of emotional connection can have significant consequences for individuals and the dynamics of relationships. In such scenarios, the transactional nature of the interactions may lead to a superficial and short-lived sense of gratification, but it often leaves a void where emotional fulfillment should reside.

The dire consequences of prioritizing physical pleasure over emotional connection can manifest in various ways. Individuals engaged in solely physical relationships may find themselves experiencing a sense of emptiness or loneliness, as the short-lived nature of these encounters fails to address the fundamental human need for emotional closeness and understanding.

Furthermore, this behavior can contribute to a cycle of dissatisfaction and a lack of fulfillment in relationships. When individuals become accustomed to separating physical pleasure from emotional connection, they may struggle to establish and maintain meaningful, long-term partnerships. This approach to intimacy can hinder the development of genuine emotional bonds, potentially leading to a pattern of short-lived and unfulfilling connections.

In summary, the pursuit of physical pleasure without a sincere desire for emotional connection can result in emotional emptiness, loneliness, and a pattern of unsatisfying relationships. It highlights the importance of recognizing and valuing both the physical and emotional dimensions of intimacy for a truly fulfilling and enduring connection.

Building Trust and Reinforcing Emotional Bond

The intimate act of couples coming together in sexual intimacy plays a profound role in building trust and reinforcing the emotional bonds that tie them together. This shared experience creates a unique space where vulnerability is embraced, and a deep sense of trust is cultivated. The exchange of body fluids, while a physical aspect, holds symbolic significance in the emotional landscape of the relationship.

Trust, a cornerstone of any healthy relationship, is nurtured through the shared vulnerability inherent in sexual intimacy. As couples expose their true selves in these moments, a foundation of trust is laid brick by brick. The act of trusting one's partner with one's most intimate self creates a sense of security, a belief that one can be open and authentic without fear of judgment.

Moreover, the exchange of body fluids during intimacy carries a symbolic weight. It represents a level of interconnectedness and shared experiences that extend beyond the physical realm. In these moments, couples are not only physically close but are also metaphorically intertwining their lives, creating a web of shared memories, emotions, and experiences. During this time, couples trust each other with a deeper understanding that extends far beyond the spoken word.

In the vulnerability of sexual intimacy, partners are invited to shed their protective layers and reveal their authentic selves. This mutual exposure creates a level of intimacy that goes beyond the surface, creating a shared emotional space where insecurities, fears, and desires are laid bare. The act of baring one's physical self becomes symbolic of baring one's soul, and in this mutual unveiling, a profound connection is forged.

The emotional bonds reinforced through sexual intimacy extend beyond the act itself, permeating various facets of the relationship. Couples who share a deep emotional connection forged in the crucible of vulnerability experience a heightened sense of understanding and empathy towards each other. This understanding becomes a source of strength during moments of disagreement or conflict.

Moreover, sexual intimacy serves as a powerful tool for communication within a relationship. It provides a unique language through which partners express love, desire, and affirmation without uttering a single word. The non-verbal communication of sexual intimacy transcends linguistic barriers, allowing couples to connect on a profound level that words alone cannot reach.

In conclusion, sexual intimacy is a multifaceted phenomenon that goes beyond physical pleasure—it is a vehicle for emotional connection, trust-building, and communication within a relationship. Understanding its profound significance and approaching it with intentionality can contribute to the development of a strong and enduring emotional bond between partners.

Chapter Two

Debunking
Myths & Misconceptions

"True intimacy thrives in an environment of authenticity and mutual understanding, elements that can be overshadowed by the disguise of sexual invincibility."

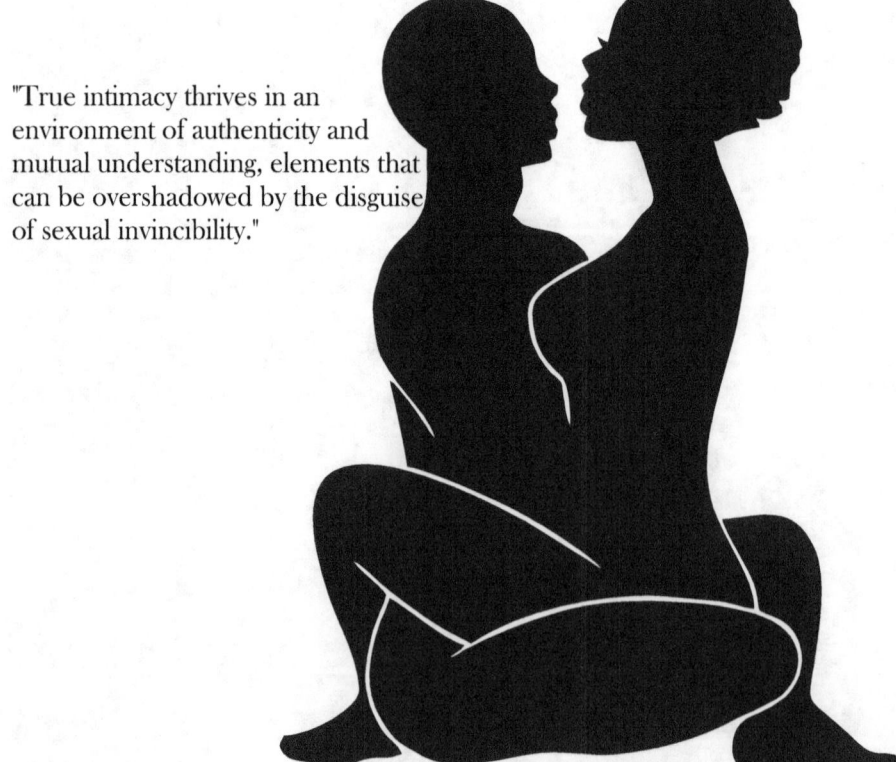

Debunking Myths & Misconceptions

Before we dive into the myths surrounding sexual intimacy, let's first grasp what myths and misconceptions are. Myths are stories or beliefs that might not be based on facts, often passed down through generations or propagated by society, serving cultural and symbolic purposes. On the other hand, misconceptions are incorrect ideas stemming from misunderstandings or misinterpretations of facts.

These myths and misconceptions about sexual intimacy are shaped by cultural, societal, and historical influences. In this chapter, we'll explore these beliefs, aiming to separate fact from fiction and provide a clearer perspective on the realities of sexual intimacy.

Social Evolution and Myths

As societies evolve, so do the interpretation and relevance of myths. Social evolution includes changes in cultural norms, values, and collective consciousness, influencing how myths are perceived in the modern era. Myths, once crucial for explaining the unknown and establishing cultural identity, undergo transformations in meaning and significance over time.

Myths served as foundational narratives for ancient civilizations, addressing existential questions and providing a moral compass. In the context of sexual intimacy, myths played a role in shaping societal attitudes, norms, behaviour, and expectations.

Evolution of Sexual Intimacy Myths

Over time, societal attitudes toward sexual intimacy have evolved, influencing the interpretation of related myths. Myths often framed sexuality within religious and cultural contexts, while modern perspectives tend to emphasize personal autonomy, consent, and diverse expressions of intimacy.

As societies undergo social evolution, individuals reinterpret myths to align with modern values. Myths continue to serve as a source of inspiration, shaping art, literature, and popular culture. In the realm of sexual intimacy, understanding the psychological context of myths becomes crucial for navigating the complexities of relationships.

The evolving understanding of myths, reflects broader societal shifts, including changes in attitudes toward sexual intimacy. By exploring the psychological context of these myths, we gain insights into the foundations that have shaped perceptions of sexuality. As we debunk sexual intimacy myths, it's essential to recognize their psychological relevance while embracing values that promote healthy, consensual, and equitable relationships.

Let's unravel the stories engraved into our understanding of sex and relationships, exploring how these myths have impacted individuals and societies.

The Myth of Newness: Debunking the Misconception that Novel Sexual Experiences are Inherently Better

I want to challenge the idea that new sexual experiences are automatically appealing, especially when it comes to sexual intimacy. By exploring the psychological factors that contribute to this belief, I encourage a nuanced understanding of desire and satisfaction. Here, I will emphasize the importance of communication and shared understanding in establishing genuine satisfaction in intimate relationships, challenging the myth that newness alone enhances pleasure.

As a relationship coach, one of my clients, Lerato, called me, she was distressed, and desperate to save her marriage which was only 4 years old. This was after the revelation about her STD diagnosis and the subsequent confrontation to her husband, Themba, who had confessed to have had unprotected sex with another woman. The couple sought my guidance to navigate the difficult aftermath. As the relationship coach, I approached the situation with a compassionate understanding of the complexities of their situation.

Addressing Themba and Lerato's predicament required a delicate balance of empathy, practicality and honesty. I began by acknowledging the pain and betrayal Lerato felt, recognizing the gravity of the situation. But I also needed to establish what was the source of Themba's behaviour. It was crucial to create a safe space for both individuals to express their emotions and concerns openly.

The coaching process involved a series of reflective exercises aimed at helping Themba understand the root of his actions and challenging the societal myth that had fueled his pursuit of new sexual experiences. We explored the pressures imposed by external expectations and discussed the importance of communication and emotional intimacy in a committed relationship.

Recognizing the impact of Themba's social circle on his choices, we delved into the need for him to reassess and redefine his friendships. Understanding that societal myths can be starved when couples embrace a deeper understanding of their sexuality, we focused on ways to improve sexual experiences and satisfaction within the bounds of their committed relationship.

One key aspect of the coaching sessions was guiding Themba and Lerato toward rebuilding trust. This involved establishing clear communication channels, encouraging transparency, and addressing the underlying issues that had contributed to Themba's infidelity. Additionally, we worked together to dispel the myth that seeking new sexual experiences is a prerequisite for a fulfilling and enduring sex life.

Throughout the process, the coaching sessions emphasized the importance of embracing authenticity, finding satisfaction within the unique dynamics of Themba and Lerato's relationship, and challenging societal myths that could jeopardize their connection.

Debunking Myths & Misconceptions

One thing I had noticed with this couple was the love they had for one another. Even though Themba had went out to seek newer sexual experiences, it was clear that he loved his wife deeply and did not want to lose her. Myths and misconceptions can lead people into doing things that has the potential to harm even that which they love the most.

Most of the time, partners would do things in secret with the hope that they will never get caught, unfortunately, the truth always finds a way of coming out. The biggest need for this couple was knowledge; their lack of understanding on sexual intimacy gravely affected their relationship.

The truth of the matter is that, Themba left his marital bed in pursuit of something he could have found on the same bed. What he went out to find was not newness, but it was feeding his curiosity. The problem was not the lack of pleasure, but it was feeding his curiosity. He had believed that the new girl would give him something his wife cannot give him, but chances are that he will still not be satisfied with the new girl and will soon be in search for another new girl.

This then becomes a very distractive circle, it sends one from one pleasure spot to another without giving you real satisfaction. The only way to break out of this circle is by firstly understanding that the honey pot is not there, but it is here with me everyday. Many individuals find themselves in the streets in pursuit of satisfaction, only to find themselves in a never ending race that ends up in heartbreak and frustration.

Sexual intimacy is like a human mind, the capacity it has is way too big compared to what we use. Sex is very broad and it has so many layers to be uncovered. We have not yet explored an inch of it, there is still so much to explore as long as we open the taps and begin communicating with our partners. This too requires openness and partners who will be willing to go out to explore this world of erotica.

Moreover, it's crucial to recognize that seeking satisfaction outside the relationship is unlikely to lead to a better experience. The grass isn't always greener on the other side, and chasing fleeting pleasures elsewhere can ultimately leave one feeling unsatisfied and unfulfilled.

In addition to creating intimacy through understanding and breaking barriers, it is imperative for couples to explore diverse avenues of pleasure. Much like a gourmet chef constantly innovates to tantalize taste buds, couples must endeavor to discover new ways to delight each other sensually. Just as consuming the same meal day in and day out would eventually dull the palate, relying on repetitive techniques in intimacy can lead to stagnation and disinterest.

Particularly noteworthy is the importance of acknowledging and addressing the differing needs between partners. Women, in particular, can become quickly disenchanted by monotony and routine. Thus, embracing newer experiences within the relationship and creativity becomes paramount in sustaining mutual satisfaction. Couples should aspire to be adventurous in their pursuit of pleasure, venturing beyond the confines of familiarity to explore uncharted territories of desire.

By embracing this mindset, couples can rise beyond limitations and embark on a journey of mutual growth and exploration. Confronting challenges together strengthens their bond and creates a deeper understanding of each other's desires and boundaries. Through this shared commitment to evolution within the relationship, couples not only enrich their experiences but also cultivate profound moments of intimacy that endure far beyond short-lived encounters.

The key lies in recognizing the potential for growth and transformation within the relationship. By actively seeking out new ways to pleasure and connect with each other, couples can forge a bond that is resilient, fulfilling, and enduring.

So, it is a myth that the only way to have a fulfilled sexual life is if you can have a side chick to pleasure yourself with. Your partner does not need a pleasure assistant, together with your partner you can create an amazing world of fulfilled sexual desires.

Navigating the Shadows: The Myth of Gender Superiority in Sexual Intimacy

This section unravels the longstanding myth of gender superiority deeply entrenched in patriarchal beliefs within the realm of sexual intimacy. It delves into the historical and cultural roots perpetuating notions of one gender being superior to the other in sexual relationships. By exploring the impact of these patriarchal beliefs on individuals and societies, the section aims to dispel the myth and encourage a more equitable and respectful approach to sexual intimacy. It emphasizes the importance of recognizing and challenging deep-seated stereotypes contributing to gender-based power imbalances in intimate relationships, guiding individuals toward creating healthier and more mutually fulfilling connections.

Examining the enduring influence of patriarchy on our perceptions of relationships, this historical belief in male superiority has cast a long shadow over societies, shaping our understanding of gender roles. From early childhood, these beliefs take root, becoming deeply ingrained in our cultural fabric.

Despite the progress of time, the influence of patriarchy persists, affecting societal norms and impacting how we approach intimate relationships. The entrenched notion of male superiority has created a power imbalance, influencing expectations and behaviors. The aim is to unearth the historical roots of these gender myths, illuminating their sustained impact. By acknowledging these historical patterns, we can actively challenge outdated beliefs and strive for relationships built on equality and mutual respect.

In different cultures, the manifestation of patriarchy varies, but its core message remains constant: the perception of men as superior and women as inferior. Uncovering the diverse expressions of patriarchy across cultures, we highlight that, while the language may differ, the practice is often the same. Understanding these variations empowers us to dismantle the oppressive structures that have persisted for generations.

Moreover, with contemporary attitudes shifting towards equality, women are no longer confined to traditional roles. The outdated notion that a woman's place is solely in the kitchen or as the primary caregiver is being dismantled. Equal opportunities in the corporate world have challenged these stereotypes, demonstrating that women are just as capable in various spheres beyond domestic duties. As societal expectations evolve, this encourages a reevaluation of gender norms, building relationships founded on shared responsibilities and genuine partnership.

Let us delve into the negative impact patriarchy had on society, affecting sexual intimacy.

1. Power Imbalance and Control

Patriarchy has historically perpetuated a power imbalance between genders, positioning men as superior and women as inferior. This power dynamic often translates into control within relationships, limiting women's autonomy and decision-making power. In the realm of sexual intimacy, this can lead to non-consensual practices, unequal fulfillment of desires, and an environment where one partner dominates the other.

2. Reinforcement of Gender Stereotypes

Patriarchal beliefs reinforce rigid gender stereotypes, prescribing specific roles and expectations for men and women. These stereotypes can significantly impact sexual intimacy by imposing unrealistic standards on both genders. Men may feel pressured to conform to hyper-masculine ideals, while women may face expectations that prioritize passivity and subservience. This can result in a lack of authentic connection and hinder the exploration of diverse and fulfilling sexual experiences.

3. Stigmatization of Female Sexuality

Patriarchy often contributes to the stigmatization of female sexuality, viewing it through a lens of shame and control. This can manifest in various ways, such as the policing of women's bodies, shaming of sexual desires, and the propagation of double standards. In sexual relationships, these attitudes can lead to inhibitions, guilt, and a reluctance to express one's desires openly. It creates an environment where women may feel the need to conform to societal expectations rather than embracing their sexuality authentically.

In the 70s, 80s, and sometimes in the 90s, many men from South African villages went to work in Johannesburg's mines, leaving their families behind. They would return home once a year to a well-kept home, and the wives would wait, having kept themselves for their husbands. However, this annual reunion was more about satisfying the man's sexual desires, with little concern for the wife's sexual needs.

During this time, women felt silenced, unable to express their sexual frustrations. Sex was mainly seen as a way to have children, and women rarely experienced pleasure. The prevailing culture, influenced by patriarchy, led to a situation where women endured intimate moments without their desires being considered.

This historical period reflects a time when gender-based oppression was widespread. The oppressive nature of patriarchy denied women control over their bodies and sexual experiences. Looking back, we see that this oppression is incompatible with the values of today's society. It highlights the progress still needed to break free from historical gender-based oppression and create relationships based on equality and mutual respect.

Moreover, in some cases, even when men were present with their families, there was often a lack of concern for the sexual satisfaction of their wives. This lack of understanding, coupled with societal standards, further oppressed women, infringing upon their rights. Shockingly, these conditions were considered normal during that era, highlighting the deeply ingrained nature of gender-based oppression and the need for societal evolution toward more equitable relationships.

In unraveling the myth of gender superiority, it becomes evident that the evolution of societal beliefs is crucial for building healthier relationships. The negative impact of patriarchy, with its power imbalances and reinforcement of gender stereotypes, calls for a collective effort to break free from these historical shackles.

As we strive for a society founded on equality and mutual respect, it is essential to recognize the transformative benefits of such a paradigm shift. Embracing an evolved mindset unlocks the potential for more authentic connections, where partners are equal contributors to their intimate experiences. The dismantling of gender-based stereotypes paves the way for genuine partnerships, unburdened by outdated expectations.

The journey toward equality in sexual intimacy is, at its core, a journey toward richer, more fulfilling relationships. It liberates individuals from the constraints of oppressive norms, allowing them to explore the depths of intimacy with open hearts and minds. Evolving beyond patriarchal beliefs not only benefits individuals but also contributes to the creation of a society where everyone is free to express their desires, preferences, and vulnerabilities without fear of judgment.

In conclusion, let us embrace the ongoing transformation towards equality and mutual respect, recognizing its power to redefine the landscape of intimate relationships. As we challenge the remnants of gender superiority, we pave the way for a future where love, connection, and understanding thrive on the principles of equality, creating a world where everyone can experience the true beauty of authentic intimacy.

Moreover, by debunking the myths of gender superiority, we create space for individuals to express themselves authentically and without constraints. This liberation allows for a deeper level of connection and understanding between partners, as they are free to explore and celebrate each other's unique qualities and desires. As we continue to dismantle outdated beliefs, we create a more inclusive and compassionate society where all individuals can experience the full richness of intimate relationships, unbound by restrictive gender norms.

In breaking free from the myth of gender superiority, we're unraveling the knots of inequality that have held back intimate relationships. The shift towards equality isn't just a journey; it's a powerful change, rewriting the story of love and connection. As we work towards a future filled with respect and understanding, let's build a world where every voice matters, every desire is valued, and every heart is free from outdated beliefs.

Beyond Perfect: Embracing Real Bodies and True Intimacy

In a world where we often see pictures of perfect bodies and get told how we should look, it's easy to forget what real bodies are like. This part of our journey is about breaking the myth that only certain bodies are beautiful, especially when it comes to being close with someone.

We'll talk about how society and what we see in the media can make us believe in a kind of beauty that's hard to achieve. But the truth is, real bodies have their own stories - stories of life, strength, and what makes each person special. Sadly, the pressure to look a certain way can make us forget to appreciate the beauty in our uniqueness.

To explain these ideas, let me share a personal story, an extract from my first book, The Paradigms of Love:

"Growing up in Turfloop, I met a young, beautiful lightskinned thick girl. This young girl had the biggest crush I have ever known on me; she couldn't hide it no matter how best she tried. Her face literally lit every time she saw me and she did things a girl can only do when she is head over heels in love with a guy.

Debunking Myths & Misconceptions

We enjoyed each other's company; we laughed and spent so much time together. Deep in my heart I knew that she was head over heels in love and to some extent I felt sorry for her because I knew I did not feel the same about her. Not that she was not lovable or pretty enough, I was just bewitched! Yeah, there I said it, I admit that I was bewitched and made to think thick girls are not sexy and they are not relationship material (If there is such). She had a beautiful personality and that was one of the reasons we spent a lot of time together. Did I mention that she was smart, too?

It's unbelievable how we miss out on love because of our psychological setup. Time and again we reject people because of our outlook and interpretation of life. To this day, philosophers still can't find the true definition of 'beautiful' and until they find a very convincing absolute definition, the tale of beauty will always be told by the eyes of the beholder."

This story reflects a common struggle – how our perceptions of beauty, often shaped by societal standards, can influence our connections and love stories.

Embarking on the journey of embracing real bodies and true intimacy is a profound exploration, especially in a world dominated by narrow beauty standards. Society's relentless emphasis on specific body ideals, perpetuated by media and societal norms, often creates an environment where many feel inadequate. In this section, we challenge these unrealistic standards, placing a spotlight on genuine appreciation for the diverse and unique stories our bodies tell, particularly within the context of sexual intimacy.

Societal norms and media representations wield significant influence, dictating a particular image of beauty that encourages unrealistic expectations. The pressure to conform to these ideals can leave individuals grappling with insecurities and self-doubt, especially when it comes to intimate connections. The journey toward embracing real bodies involves navigating the impact of these standards on our self-esteem and relationships.

My realization that I had been swayed by societal standards serves as a reminder of how these norms can hinder genuine connections. The story I shared challenges the quest for a universal definition of beauty, asserting that it will always reside in the eyes of the beholder.

The journey toward embracing real bodies and true intimacy places a spotlight on the unique stories engraved into our bodies, especially in the context of sexual connection. It champions the uniqueness of each individual, creating a paradigm shift away from rigid beauty standards. By celebrating our distinct narratives, we create space for authentic connections built on acceptance, understanding, and the profound beauty found in our individuality.

At the heart of embracing real bodies and true intimacy lies the profound journey of self-acceptance. In a world that often scrutinizes and critiques our appearances, learning to love and appreciate oneself becomes a radical act. The path to true intimacy begins with acknowledging and embracing our bodies, recognizing the unique beauty and stories they carry. Self-acceptance becomes the foundation upon which authentic connections can flourish, unburdened by insecurities and societal pressures.

It is often said that the greatest love one can receive is the love they cultivate for themselves. This foundational love acts as a compass, guiding individuals towards a deeper understanding of their worth and inherent beauty. When we wholeheartedly accept ourselves, imperfections and all, we pave the way for meaningful connections with others. The journey toward true intimacy becomes a reciprocal exchange of love, where the authenticity of each individual contributes to a shared narrative of acceptance, understanding, and genuine connection.

As we conclude our exploration into the myth of perfection in physical appearance, let these words serve as a gentle reminder: the canvas of intimacy is painted with the vibrant hues of authenticity, not the muted tones of societal expectations. Embracing real bodies and true intimacy is an invitation to break free from the chains of perfectionism and celebrate the diverse beauty that resides within each of us.

In a world where every scar, curve, and nuance tells a story, we encourage you to step into the realm of self-love and acceptance. Shed the weight of unrealistic standards, for the greatest masterpiece is the one that reflects the truth of who you are. As you embark on this journey, remember that true intimacy blossoms in the garden of authenticity, where imperfections are cherished, and genuine connections are cultivated.

So, dear reader, embrace the artistry of your being, and let the masterpiece of self-love resonate in every intimate encounter. The canvas awaits your unique strokes, painting a world where beauty is defined by the authenticity that radiates from within.

Unveiling the Illusions: Deconstructing Myths Propagated by Pornography

In the complex world of intimacy, couples often find themselves influenced by factors beyond their shared moments. One significant influence is the world of pornography, creating illusions that can profoundly affect relationships. Whether both partners are drawn in or only one grapples with its grip, the consequences are real, leaving a void that may go unnoticed until it strains the connection.

As we delve into the myths and misconceptions of pornography, aiming to shed light on its unsuspecting influence. Through a candid conversation, we'll navigate the complexities introduced by explicit content, exploring challenges when both partners are affected and the nuances of relationships where one struggles with its allure.

Before we embark on our conversation, let's take a moment to unravel the concept of pornography and distinguish between the illusions it presents and the reality it often overlooks.

In Illusion: In the realm of illusion, pornography unfolds as a carefully curated fantasy, meticulously crafted to stimulate arousal. It paints a distorted picture of sexual intimacy, emphasizing performance over authenticity and scripted scenarios over genuine connection. The actors become vessels for desire, their experiences molded to fit a predetermined narrative that seldom aligns with the complexities of real-world relationships.

In Reality: Conversely, the real-world dynamics of intimacy involve a spectrum of emotions, vulnerabilities, and genuine expressions of love and desire. It's important to recognize that the hyper-stylized portrayals in pornography are a far cry from the authentic, imperfect beauty of human connections. The richness of intimacy lies in the nuances of shared moments, mutual understanding, and the unique dance between partners.

Behind the Scenes: It's crucial to acknowledge that the performers in pornographic content often grapple with the use of drugs to sustain their on-screen performance. This reliance on substances to meet unrealistic standards highlights the stark contrast between the artificial nature of pornography and the natural, unenhanced experiences of real-world intimacy.

Attempting to replicate the scenarios depicted in adult entertainment, which are often fueled by external substances, can place undue pressure on individuals and strain the authenticity of their connections. As we navigate the impact of pornography on your relationship, remember that the standards set by an industry dependent on artificial enhancements may not align with the healthy and sustainable dynamics of a genuine, drug-free relationship.

Let us look into the relationship of Mpho and Rhulani:

Mpho and Rhulani's Unspoken Struggle: A Conversation

(It has been some time that Mpho and Rulani have been married and they soon felt a need to enhance their sexual lives. They struggled to enjoy their intimate moments and thus they felt that their relationship is threatened.)

Mpho: *Rhulani, I was thinking... you know, maybe we could try something new in the bedroom. I've heard people say that watching pornography can spice things up.*

Rhulani: *Oh, um, I guess we could give it a try. It might be fun...*

(As Mpho and Rhulani delve into the world of adult entertainment, their initial excitement soon transforms into a silent struggle. The scenes they witness on screen become benchmarks, setting unrealistic expectations that cast shadows over their intimate moments. The spontaneity and genuine connection they once shared start to erode as the pressure to emulate the performances in pornography intensifies.)

Mpho: *Rhulani, do you think we're doing it right? I mean, compared to what we see in those movies?*

Rhulani: *I don't know, Mpho. It just feels like we're not measuring up to what they show. Maybe we're not doing something we should be doing?*

(In a subsequent encounter, Rhulani begins to express deeper concerns about their intimate moments.)

Rhulani: *Mpho, I've been thinking. It feels like our intimate moments lack something. It's like you're trying to perform rather than connecting with me. I want us to be close, to share something meaningful, and not just recreate scenes from those movies.*

Mpho: *Oh, I didn't realize you felt that way. I just wanted to try something different, you know, to make things exciting.*

Rhulani: *But, Mpho, it's not exciting when it feels like you're not really present. It's as if you're more focused on being the star of the show more than being with me. I want us to be intimate in a way that respects and connects with both of us, not just for the sake of performance.*

In their attempt to enhance their intimate life, Mpho and Rhulani find themselves ensnared in the web of comparison and frustration. The initial intention to explore something new has inadvertently become a source of tension, leaving them questioning their own adequacy and the authenticity of their connection.

As couples navigate the tumultuous terrain influenced by pornography, various distressing scenarios may unfold. One challenging path involves the introduction of a third party into their intimate space. Drawn by the illusion of heightened pleasure portrayed in adult films, a partner may express the desire to include another person in their encounters, believing it will add excitement and novelty.

The influence of adult entertainment can distort perceptions of what constitutes a fulfilling intimate relationship. The introduction of a third party, often stemming from the desire to recreate on-screen fantasies, can lead to complications and emotional turmoil. It may strain the bonds of trust, creating a wedge between partners who initially sought to enhance their connection.

In more distressing scenarios, the impact of pornography may drive a partner to seek fulfillment outside the relationship. Frustrated by unmet expectations and influenced by the often unrealistic and sensationalized portrayals in adult films, an individual might succumb to the misguided belief that satisfaction lies beyond the boundaries of their committed partnership.

This perilous journey into infidelity can be fueled by a misguided quest for the unattainable highs depicted in adult content. The gap between fantasy and reality widens, leading to a sense of desperation and a search for gratification in unconventional avenues. The emotional fallout is profound, as trust shatters, and the foundation of the relationship crumbles under the weight of unmet desires and distorted expectations.

These scenarios underscore the dangerous consequences of allowing the influence of pornography to permeate the dynamics of a relationship. The pursuit of illusory pleasures, whether through the inclusion of third parties or seeking satisfaction elsewhere, can jeopardize the very core of a once-loving connection, leaving partners grappling with the wreckage of shattered trust and broken intimacy.

In wrapping up, it's crucial to realize that thinking pornography can enhance relationships is a dangerous myth. It might seem like a fun idea, but it often brings more harm than good. Instead of bringing couples closer, it can create problems like unrealistic expectations and a distorted view of real intimacy.

Couples need to be careful when considering this, understanding the huge gap between scripted fantasies in adult content and the complex reality of genuine relationships. The risks of introducing pornography into intimate moments, whether due to unrealistic expectations or seeking external thrills, are more significant than any brief excitement.

Real intimacy is built on communication, empathy, and a true connection between partners. Rather than relying on outside influences, couples should explore each other's desires, talk openly about their needs, and build trust and respect. By steering clear of the false promises of pornography, couples can build a foundation rooted in reality, leading to a more satisfying and enduring connection.

Debunking the Superhero Myth

In the world of intimacy, the superhero mindset can take hold, where individuals see themselves as flawless sexual beings. This outlook, however, can be a stumbling block to genuine connection. The belief that one is already a master in the art of intimacy may prevent the openness needed for mutual exploration and understanding. We delve into the unrealistic expectations and pressures associated with this perception, emphasizing the importance of embracing authenticity and acknowledging the complexities of real bodies and sexual experiences.

The section encourages a more grounded and compassionate approach to intimacy, moving away from the idealized superhero narrative often fueled by societal norms and media influences.

Every intimate encounter is like a new chapter, a unique story waiting to unfold. Approaching it with humility, recognizing that there's always something new to learn about our partner and ourselves, is the key to breaking free from the superhero myth. It's not about perfection; it's about the beautiful dance of discovering and embracing the nuances that make each intimate connection special.

Here, we'll unravel the superhero myth, urging everyone to embrace a more humble and open approach to intimacy. Let's celebrate the uniqueness of each encounter, where vulnerability is not a weakness but a powerful force that strengthens the bonds of connection.

The superhero myth takes center stage, portraying individuals as flawless sexual beings. The idea that one has mastered the art of intimacy can, unfortunately, hinder rather than enhance the connection between partners. The belief in sexual perfection often brings with it a set of detrimental consequences that can cast a shadow over the authentic experience of intimacy.

1. Erosion of Open Communication

When an individual sees themselves as a sexual superhero, there's a risk of closing the door to open communication. The assumption that one already knows everything there is to know about intimacy may lead to a lack of curiosity and a diminishing willingness to understand their partner's evolving desires and preferences. This erosion of open communication can create a disconnect between partners, hindering the potential for shared growth and exploration.

2. Ignoring the Uniqueness of Each Encounter

Intimacy is not a one-size-fits-all experience. Each encounter is a unique interplay of emotions, desires, and individual nuances. The superhero mentality, however, tends to overlook this uniqueness. Partners may miss out on the opportunity to fully appreciate and engage in the beauty of every intimate moment when trapped in the belief that a predetermined set of skills is sufficient for all situations.

3. Strain on Authentic Connection

The superhero myth can place undue pressure on maintaining an image of perfection, leading to a strained and inauthentic connection between partners. The fear of vulnerability, making mistakes, or expressing needs and desires can hinder the development of a deeper, more meaningful bond. True intimacy thrives in an environment of authenticity and mutual understanding, elements that can be overshadowed by the facade of sexual invincibility.

4. Resistance to Growth and Learning

A superhero believes they've reached the pinnacle of their abilities, leaving little room for growth or learning. In the context of intimacy, this resistance to new experiences and knowledge can stagnate the evolution of a couple's sexual connection. The journey of exploration and shared discovery is a continuous process, and the belief in sexual perfection can impede this natural and enriching progression.

Connecting with an individual wrapped in the cape of sexual superheroism can be akin to attempting to breach an impenetrable fortress. The walls erected by their perceived invincibility and flawless prowess create a barrier that can impede genuine connection.

This is because sexual superheroes often find themselves shielded by the armor of self-absorption. The belief in their infallibility can create a self-centered approach to intimacy, where their focus is predominantly on showcasing their perceived skills rather than engaging in a reciprocal exchange of emotions and desires. This self-absorption erects a barrier that makes it challenging for their partner to feel seen, heard, and truly connected.

The pursuit of perfection can also transform intimacy into a performance rather than a shared experience. Sexual superheroes may become so fixated on meeting an idealized standard that they lose sight of the authentic, imperfect beauty of connection. Partners can feel alienated by the relentless quest for flawless execution, yearning for moments of vulnerability and genuine shared experiences instead.

Genuine connection thrives on emotional intimacy, a terrain where vulnerability, empathy, and shared experiences intertwine. The superhero mentality, however, tends to prioritize physical prowess over emotional connection. As a result, partners may struggle to penetrate the emotional walls erected by the superhero, leaving the relationship devoid of the depth and richness that emotional intimacy can provide.

Amidst the allure of superhuman sexual feats, it's essential to underscore the profound importance of connection. True intimacy transcends the superficiality of perceived perfection, finding its roots in authentic shared moments, emotional resonance, and a deep understanding of each other's desires. The quest for a connection that goes beyond the facade

Debunking Myths & Misconceptions

of superheroic abilities becomes paramount for cultivating a relationship that stands the test of time.

As we delve deeper into this exploration, we'll unravel strategies to break through the walls of sexual superheroism, creating an environment where connection takes precedence over the pursuit of mythical perfection. The journey towards authentic intimacy invites partners to embrace vulnerability, communicate openly, and celebrate the imperfect beauty that lies at the heart of genuine connection.

Here are some strategies for bridging the gap and embracing connection over mythical perfection:

Open Communication

Initiate honest and open conversations about intimacy, desires, and expectations. Encourage a safe space where both partners can express their feelings without judgment. This lays the foundation for understanding each other's needs and dispelling the notion of a perfect sexual script.

Vulnerability as Strength

Promote the idea that vulnerability is a strength, not a weakness. Break down the barriers of superheroic invincibility by embracing the imperfections that make each person unique. Share personal experiences, desires, and fears to create a more genuine and intimate connection.

Mutual Exploration

Approach intimacy as a mutual exploration rather than a performance. Focus on discovering each other's preferences, trying new things together, and adapting to the ebb and flow of desires. This collaborative approach encourages a sense of partnership, steering away from the one-sided superhero narrative.

Prioritize Emotional Connection

Highlight the importance of emotional connection in encouraging a healthy and satisfying intimate relationship. Shift the focus from physical feats to emotional resonance, encouraging partners to be attuned to each other's feelings, building a deeper connection beyond the superficial.

Educate and Learn Together

Acknowledge that everyone is constantly evolving, and there's always room to learn and grow. Explore educational resources together, attend workshops or read literature on intimacy as a couple. This shared learning experience can break down the egoistic barriers and create a collaborative journey.

Establish Shared Goals

Work together to establish shared goals for your intimate life. These goals should be centered around connection, communication, and shared pleasure rather than conforming to external standards. Setting joint intentions creates a sense of unity and purpose in your intimate relationship.

Seek Professional Guidance

If the walls of sexual superheroism prove challenging to dismantle, consider seeking the guidance of a relationship or sex therapist. Professional assistance can provide a neutral space for both partners to express themselves and receive expert advice on creating a more connected and fulfilling intimate life.

Breaking through the walls of sexual superheroism requires a concerted effort from both partners. By prioritizing open communication, vulnerability, and shared exploration, couples can pave the way for a more authentic and connected intimate relationship, free from the constraints of mythical perfection.

Debunking Myths & Misconceptions

In the realm of intimate connections, the superhero myth imposes unrealistic expectations that hinder genuine connection and shared pleasure. The belief in perfect sexual prowess can create a barrier between partners, hindering the exploration of true intimacy. However, breaking free from this myth is not only possible but essential for encouraging a more authentic and fulfilling connection.

As we navigate the complexities of intimate relationships, it's crucial to acknowledge that perfection is a myth. Each person is unique, with individual desires, preferences, and experiences. Embracing imperfection becomes a powerful tool for cultivating a deeper connection, as it allows partners to be genuine and vulnerable with each other.

True intimacy thrives in an environment where partners recognize and celebrate each other's flaws and imperfections. It is the shared journey of exploration, learning, and mutual understanding that truly defines a satisfying intimate relationship. Rather than striving for an unattainable ideal, couples can find joy and fulfillment in the authenticity of their connection.

So, let us shed the cape of perfection and embrace the beautifully imperfect nature of our intimate selves. In doing so, we open the door to a richer, more meaningful connection, free from the constraints of superhero expectations. Remember, the real magic happens when two imperfect beings come together, creating a unique and beautiful dance of intimacy that transcends the limitations of mythical perfection.

Debunking the Size Myths: Real Talk about Size in Intimacy

In the world of intimacy, there are myths that mistakenly connect physical attributes to desirability. One prevalent misconception centers around the belief that a man's worth is tied to the size of his penis, creating unnecessary insecurities and distorting the true essence of connection. Similarly, there's an unfounded notion about vaginal tightness determining a woman's allure. This myth encourages unrealistic expectations, overshadowing the genuine elements crucial for a fulfilling and satisfying intimate relationship.

In this open conversation, we aim to debunk these size myths, challenging harmful narratives and emphasizing that desirability goes beyond physical dimensions. Our exploration focuses on embracing diversity, appreciating individual uniqueness, and building genuine understanding as the foundation of an enriching and authentic connection. Let's break free from stereotypes, reject unrealistic expectations, and celebrate the varied experiences that contribute to the variety of intimate relationships.

Let us navigate through the complexities of size myths, providing insights and perspectives for a healthier, more compassionate approach to intimacy. Together, we'll uncover the realities, promote acceptance, and pave the way for relationships grounded in mutual understanding and genuine connection.

It's about time we dispel the notion that big is inherently better and that small is something to be ashamed of. Size is just a physical attribute, not a measure of worth or desirability. It's crucial to understand that big is big, and small is small – neither is a reflection of a person's value. Instead, it's about how one approaches and values the unique aspects of their body.

For those blessed with a larger size, it's essential to recognize the responsibility that comes with it. While a bigger stature can bring advantages in certain contexts, it's not a guarantee of superior performance. In fact, it demands more care and sensitivity, considering the potential risks associated with a larger manhood. Intimacy is about connection, not causing discomfort. The fragility of the woman's anatomy requires thoughtful handling to ensure a positive experience.

On the other hand, a smaller penis should never be a source of shame. There are distinct advantages to a smaller size, such as requiring less sensitivity. This can lead to prolonged and mutually satisfying experiences without the need for excessive caution. Small doesn't equate to inferior – it's about understanding and embracing the unique dynamics that smaller dimensions can bring to the intimate journey.

Let us move beyond the stereotypes, acknowledging that size is just one aspect of the diverse world that makes each person unique. It's time to appreciate the individuality each person brings to the table, creating a mindset that prioritizes communication, connection, and shared pleasure over societal misconceptions.

On the other hand, one pervasive and damaging myth revolves around the tightness of a woman's vagina. This myth, steeped in societal misconceptions and unfounded judgments, has led to the unfortunate shaming of women based on unrealistic expectations and uninformed beliefs.

The tightness of a vagina has been unfairly linked to assumptions about a woman's sexual history and practices. The erroneous idea that a tighter vagina signifies restraint and limited sexual activity, while a looser one suggests promiscuity, is not only unfounded but also perpetuates harmful stereotypes. In reality, the tightness or looseness of a vagina is not a reliable indicator of a person's sexual behavior or choices.

It's crucial to debunk the myth that a tight vagina is a static characteristic. In truth, the supposed tightness of the vaginal canal is a dynamic quality that can change based on various factors, with one significant factor being arousal or weak pelvic floor muscles. When a woman is sexually aroused, her body produces more lubrication, providing a slippery texture that might be misinterpreted as increased size.

Moreover, it's essential to recognize that the pelvic floor can also play a significant role in vaginal tightness or looseness. The strength and tone of the pelvic floor muscles can impact the sensation of tightness in the vaginal canal. Weak pelvic floor muscles might contribute to a feeling of looseness, while strong and well-conditioned pelvic floor muscles can enhance vaginal tone.

Several factors can contribute to weakened pelvic floor muscles. Pregnancy and childbirth, especially vaginal delivery, can stretch and strain these muscles, leading to decreased tone. Chronic constipation, which requires straining during bowel movements, can also weaken the pelvic floor over time. Additionally, hormonal changes during menopause may result in muscle atrophy and reduced pelvic floor strength. Furthermore, lifestyle factors such as obesity and high-impact activities without proper pelvic floor support can exacerbate muscle weakness. Recognizing these potential causes is vital in addressing pelvic floor health and maintaining vaginal tone.

Thankfully, addressing pelvic floor muscle strength is possible through specific exercises such as Kegels. These exercises target the muscles supporting the pelvic organs, including those around the vaginal opening, aiding in tightening and improving overall vaginal tone. Thus, instead of attributing vaginal tightness solely to sexual history or activity, understanding the influence of pelvic floor health and the potential for improvement through exercises is crucial.

This natural response to arousal highlights the misconception that vaginal tightness is a consistent and unchanging trait. A woman may experience variations in tightness, not due to her sexual history, but rather influenced by factors such as arousal levels, hydration, and overall health.

It's essential to emphasize that there is no universal standard for vaginal tightness. The idea that a tighter vagina is superior or preferable is not only inaccurate but also contributes to the unjust and unwarranted judgment of women. Every woman's body is unique, and the notion of comparing or categorizing based on uninformed standards is not only misleading but also harmful.

It's time to break free from damaging stereotypes and create an environment that celebrates diversity, acknowledging that every woman's body is uniquely her own, free from judgment and preconceived notions.

As we delve into the repercussions of the size myth on both men and women, it becomes evident that societal expectations and stereotypes surrounding intimate attributes can have profound impacts on individuals' self-esteem, relationships, and overall well-being. The pervasive belief that bigger is inherently better, coupled with unfounded assumptions about women's sexuality, contributes to a culture of unrealistic expectations.

We aim to illuminate the potential harms of the size myth, examining its effects on body image, performance pressure, relationship dynamics, and the overall mental and emotional health of individuals. In exploring these aspects, we will also unravel strategies for creating a more compassionate environment that embraces diversity, challenges harmful myths, and prioritizes open communication and acceptance in the realm of intimacy.

Let us journey toward dispelling damaging narratives and cultivating a healthier, more inclusive perspective on human bodies and intimate connections.

The ramifications of size myths extend beyond the physical realm, influencing both men and women and permeating the emotional and psychological aspects of intimate relationships. For men, the societal pressure to conform to a certain standard of size can result in feelings of inadequacy and diminished self-worth. This, in turn, may lead to performance anxiety, hindering their ability to fully engage and connect with their partners.

On the other side, women may internalize the harmful notion that their desirability is contingent on the tightness of their vagina, leading to insecurity and anxiety. The perpetuation of these myths can create a toxic cycle of unrealistic expectations, eroding the foundation of genuine connection. It is imperative to recognize the psychological toll these myths take and emphasize that true intimacy transcends physical attributes, promoting an environment of acceptance, understanding, and mutual respect.

In closing, let us debunk the size myths that pervade our perceptions of intimacy. The belief that bigger is better and tighter is superior undermines the essence of authentic connection. Embracing diversity, recognizing the unique qualities each individual brings to the intimate journey, and encouraging open communication are the keys to unlocking a fulfilling and satisfying connection. Size is not a measure of worth or desirability; it's about understanding, respecting, and celebrating the diverse expressions of intimacy that contribute to the mosaic of human connection. Let us dismantle these myths, promoting a mindset grounded in acceptance, compassion, and the celebration of genuine connection.

Shattering Taboos: Demystifying the Sacred Cow of Sex

Throughout history, talking about sex has been hush-hush, hidden away in the corners of cultural consciousness. Societies have treated discussions on this topic with a mix of reverence and discomfort, making it a secret, sacred matter. This attitude, instilled from childhood, leaves a lasting impact as individuals grow into adulthood. Moreover, gender dynamics further complicate the dialogue around sex, often silencing women and marginalizing their voices in intimate discussions.

In this exploration, we peel back the layers of tradition, cultural norms, and gender biases that have kept sex veiled in secrecy. Our goal is to challenge these long-standing taboos, creating a space where open, honest discussions about sex can flourish, free from historical constraints and unaffected by gender hierarchies. Let us embark on this journey as we break down the barriers around the sacred cow of sex, paving the way for a more liberated and informed conversation on this fundamental aspect of human existence.

Debunking Myths & Misconceptions

Throughout history, the silent treatment surrounding discussions on sex has not only been a cultural norm but also a source of frustration and anxiety for partners. The reluctance to communicate openly about intimate matters often leaves individuals grappling with unaddressed questions, concerns, and desires. The weight of societal expectations and gender dynamics further intensifies the frustration, particularly impacting women who have historically been silenced in the realm of sexual discourse.

In this section, we unravel the layers of silence that shroud the sacred cow of sex, exploring the impact of unspoken expectations, anxiety, and the pressing need for open communication in intimate relationships. Let us navigate through the complexities of breaking the silence, paving the way for healthier, more transparent conversations around this essential facet of human connection.

The silence surrounding sexual intimacy is rife from the family level onwards. Parents often fail to talk to their children about sexuality, fearing that open communication might lead to early sexual encounters. This silence, however, affects children who often learn about sexual intimacy from their peers, who also tiptoe around the subject. Eventually, children grow to be secretive about their sexuality as well, making it difficult to identify instances of abuse.

Communication stands as the cornerstone of any thriving relationship. Open and honest dialogue cultivates understanding, strengthens emotional bonds, and encourages a sense of security between partners. It provides a platform for sharing thoughts, feelings, and desires, creating a mutual space where both individuals feel heard and valued. In the absence of effective communication, relationships can become susceptible to misunderstandings, unmet needs, and a gradual erosion of the intimate connection that binds two people together.

When it comes to sexual intimacy, the significance of communication cannot be overstated. Partners engaging in open conversations about their desires, boundaries, and preferences create an environment where both can feel acknowledged and respected. This transparency builds trust and deepens the emotional connection between individuals. Verbal and non-verbal cues become guiding lights, ensuring that each partner is attuned to the other's needs, leading to a more fulfilling and satisfying experience.

Without this crucial dialogue, sexual encounters may become riddled with uncertainty, unexpressed desires, and a lack of synchronization that can hinder the overall satisfaction and fulfillment derived from intimate moments. Miscommunication or the absence of communication altogether can lead to frustration and dissatisfaction, creating a barrier to true intimacy. In contrast, when partners openly communicate their desires and boundaries, they empower each other to explore their sexuality in a safe and mutually satisfying way.

In the journey of sexual connection, communication acts as the compass, guiding partners toward shared pleasure, understanding, and an enriched bond. It paves the way for exploration and growth, allowing individuals to express themselves authentically and without fear of judgment. Through honest and open communication, partners not only enhance their physical connection but also deepen their emotional intimacy, creating a strong foundation for a fulfilling and lasting relationship.

Creating open communication in matters of sexual intimacy is essential for cultivating a healthy and satisfying partnership. It is through dialogue and mutual understanding that individuals can navigate the complexities of intimacy, ensuring that both partners feel valued, respected, and fulfilled in their shared experiences. By embracing communication as a cornerstone of their relationship, couples can embark on a journey of exploration and connection, enriching their bond and deepening their love for each other.

Unraveling the Soulmate Myth: Beyond the Illusion of Perfect Matches

The concept of soulmates has long captured the human imagination, serving as a beacon of hope in the quest for love and companionship. From ancient mythology to modern romance novels, the idea of finding one's perfect match, destined by fate or divine intervention, has been romanticized and idealized. The soulmate myth suggests that there exists a single person in the world who is our perfect counterpart, our "other half," with whom we are destined to share an unbreakable bond of love and understanding.

In popular culture, soulmates are often depicted as two individuals who effortlessly complement each other, completing each other's sentences, thoughts, and desires. They are portrayed as finding each other against all odds, overcoming obstacles and challenges to be together, and living happily ever after in a state of eternal bliss. Many people have this idea of soulmates, which has become a big part of how we think about love and relationships.

Many people yearn for this mysterious soulmate, believing that finding this perfect match will bring fulfillment, happiness, and a sense of completeness. They search for signs and synchronicities, hoping to encounter their soulmate in chance encounters, serendipitous moments, or through the guidance of fate. The belief in soulmates can be comforting, offering solace in times of loneliness or heartbreak, and providing a sense of purpose and meaning to the journey of love.

However, the soulmate myth comes with its own set of pitfalls and misconceptions. By idealizing the concept of soulmates, people may place unrealistic expectations on their partners and relationships, expecting them to fulfill all their emotional, spiritual, and physical needs effortlessly. This can lead to disappointment and disillusionment when real-life relationships fail to meet these high standards.

Moreover, the belief in soulmates can raise a passive approach to relationships, where individuals wait for their perfect match to magically appear rather than actively engaging in the process of building and nurturing meaningful connections. It can also perpetuate a sense of entitlement, where people believe they are entitled to a perfect partner who will cater to their every whim and desire.

In reality, human relationships are complex and multifaceted, shaped by a multitude of factors including compatibility, communication, shared values, and mutual respect. Rather than seeking a perfect match, it is more fruitful to focus on cultivating healthy, loving relationships based on mutual understanding, acceptance, and growth. True intimacy and connection are not defined by finding a soulmate, but by the willingness to work through challenges, support each other's growth, and cherish the imperfect beauty of human connection.

As we unravel this myth, let us embrace the richness of imperfect, yet meaningful, connections in the realm of love and intimacy. By letting go of unrealistic expectations and embracing the complexities of human relationships, we can forge deeper connections that bring joy, fulfillment, and genuine companionship into our lives.

Finally

In conclusion, debunking myths and misconceptions surrounding sexual intimacy is essential for ensuring healthier attitudes and behaviors. These myths not only shape our perceptions of ourselves and our partners but also have profound psychological impacts, often leading to feelings of inadequacy, shame, and anxiety. By challenging these misconceptions, we liberate ourselves from the constraints of unrealistic expectations and open the door to a world of increased pleasure and enjoyment.

Embracing the freedom that comes with debunking these myths allows us to explore intimacy with a sense of curiosity and openness. It enables us to prioritize communication, consent, and mutual respect, laying the foundation for deeper connections and more fulfilling experiences.

By liberating ourselves from these myths and misconceptions, we open ourselves up to a whole new world of sexual intimacy. No longer bound by the constraints of societal expectations or unrealistic standards, we can explore and celebrate the diversity of human sexuality. We discover that there is no one-size-fits-all approach to intimacy, and that true fulfillment comes from embracing our unique desires and preferences.

In this newfound freedom, we can embark on a journey of self-discovery and exploration, discovering new pleasures and depths of connection with ourselves and our partners. We learn to communicate openly and authentically, cultivating relationships built on trust, mutual respect, and shared vulnerability. With each step away from the confines of myth and misconception, we step closer to a more liberated, fulfilling, and empowered experience of sexual intimacy.

Let us continue to challenge the status quo, dismantle damaging narratives, and create a future where sexual intimacy is celebrated as a beautiful and enriching aspect of the human experience.

Chapter Three

Common
Challenges
in Sexual Intimacy

"Inability to communicate openly and honestly about needs and emotions can leave both partners feeling isolated and unheard."

Common Challenges In Sexual Intimacy

As we transition from dispelling myths and misconceptions about sexual intimacy, we step into the realm of real-world challenges that couples often confront in their close relationships. Viewed through the lens of a relationship coach, this chapter delves into the complexities of sexual intimacy, addressing common issues individuals and couples face.

By acknowledging and understanding these challenges, we open the door to constructive solutions and deeper connections in intimacy. Let us navigate the twists and turns of sexual relationships, offering practical advice to overcome obstacles and build meaningful connections. We aim to shed light on the struggles many couples encounter in their intimate lives, from communication difficulties to performance anxiety and desire discrepancies.

Through exploration and discussion, we seek to empower couples with practical strategies and insights to navigate these challenges successfully. Our ultimate goal is to have a deeper understanding of the nuances of sexual relationships and provide individuals with the tools they need to cultivate fulfilling and satisfying connections with their partners.

Now, let's dive into the common challenges individuals and couples face in the realm of sexual intimacy:

a. Desire Difference:

One of the most prevalent hurdle couples encounter is the difference in sexual desire between partners. This difference can spark feelings of frustration, resentment, and inadequacy, potentially straining the relationship.

Desire Difference is like navigating through a maze with different starting points and pathways for each partner. One may feel a strong urge for sexual connection, while the other might not share the same level of interest or frequency. This difference can create a sense of imbalance and frustration, as one partner may feel rejected or undesired, while the other may feel pressured or guilty for not meeting their partner's expectations.

The partner with higher sexual desire may feel unfulfilled, longing for more intimacy and connection, while the partner with lower desire may feel overwhelmed or pressured to engage in sexual activities they're not genuinely interested in. This dynamic can lead to a cycle of misunderstanding and conflict, where both partners struggle to find a middle ground that satisfies their needs and desires.

Moreover, Desire Differences can also affect the emotional connection between partners. The partner with higher desire may interpret their partner's lack of interest as a sign of disconnection or lack of love, leading to feelings of rejection and insecurity. On the other hand, the partner with lower desire may feel guilty or inadequate for not being able to fulfill their partner's needs, causing them to withdraw emotionally from the relationship.

Other Differences

Sipho, one of my coaching clients recently experienced a profound loss with the passing of his mother, plunging him into a deep emotional turmoil. He took a break from work and the bustling city life to care for his mother, who was hospitalized. However, amidst the chaos of arranging medical care and processing his emotions, communication between Sipho and his girlfriend Lucy faltered. Lucy, feeling disconnected and abandoned, struggled to understand the strain Sipho was under.

As Sipho's mother's health declined, the emotional distance between him and Lucy widened. When his mother eventually passed away, Sipho found himself overwhelmed with grief and the responsibilities of arranging the funeral. Lucy, unable to grasp the magnitude of Sipho's grief, confronted him, feeling neglected and unloved. Despite Sipho's attempts to explain his emotional state and the weight of his responsibilities, Lucy continued to feel overlooked.

In turn, Sipho felt unsupported and misunderstood by Lucy, exacerbating his emotional turmoil. The conflict between grieving for his mother and fulfilling his commitment to his partner weighed heavily on him. Feeling isolated and unsupported by Lucy, Sipho began to withdraw emotionally, focusing his energy on mourning his mother's loss. The growing divide between them deepened the rift in their relationship, leaving Sipho feeling neglected and Lucy feeling unappreciated.

The situation highlighted significant discrepancies in communication and understanding between Sipho and Lucy. Sipho was grappling with profound grief and overwhelming responsibilities, causing him to prioritize his emotional needs and familial obligations. However, Lucy struggled to comprehend the depth of Sipho's emotions and the magnitude of his responsibilities. Her inability to empathize with Sipho's situation led to feelings of neglect and resentment, exacerbating the strain on their relationship.

Moreover, the differing coping mechanisms employed by Sipho and Lucy further widened the emotional gap between them. While Sipho sought solace in mourning his mother's loss and managing funeral arrangements, Lucy's attempts to seek validation and support from Sipho went unfulfilled. This differences in coping strategies compounded their emotional disconnect, leaving both partners feeling isolated and misunderstood.

The lack of effective communication and mutual understanding exacerbated the rift in their relationship, highlighting the importance of addressing differences in emotional expression and support within intimate partnerships. Without a determined effort to bridge these gaps and cultivate empathy and understanding, the relationship faced the risk of further deterioration.

The central challenge Sipho faced was his uncertainty about relying on Lucy's emotional support in the future, which cast doubt on their long-term prospects as a couple. He struggled with the idea of being in a relationship with someone he perceived as lacking empathy and being selfish. Conversely, Lucy, who tends to be clingy, felt unloved and misunderstood, interpreting Sipho's lack of communication as a sign that he no longer desired to be with her. This difference in their perceptions and needs created a significant barrier to their relationship's growth and stability.

As I intervened to help Sipho and Lucy navigate through their communication breakdown and emotional discrepancies. I emphasized the importance of having effective communication skills and cultivating an attitude of mutual understanding and empathy. I encouraged them to openly express their feelings and perspectives, while actively listening to each other without judgment.

Additionally, I suggested that they explore methods to support each other's emotional needs, acknowledging the unique ways in which they both cope with challenges. By encouraging empathy and compassion in their relationship, Sipho and Lucy could bridge the emotional gap between them and work towards a stronger, more fulfilling connection.

So, understanding our differences can play a huge role in preserving our relationships and addressing the differences that often haunt relationships. It is crucial to recognize that unresolved differences can significantly impact a couple's sexual life and lead to the emergence of rifts within the relationship.

When left unattended, these differences can manifest as feelings of frustration, resentment, and emotional distance, ultimately affecting the intimate connection between partners. This can result in a decline in sexual satisfaction, decreased desire for intimacy, and even potential conflicts in the bedroom.

Therefore, acknowledging and addressing these issues head-on is essential for maintaining a healthy and fulfilling sexual relationship. By openly discussing concerns, exploring underlying emotions, and working together to find mutually satisfying solutions, couples can strengthen their bond and cultivate a more satisfying sexual connection.

b. Communication Breakdown:

Inadequate communication surrounding sexual needs, desires, and boundaries can erect barriers to intimacy, hindering the ability to forge deeper connections and understand each other's needs.

Sipho and Lucy's story vividly demonstrates the consequences of poor communication within a relationship. As Sipho grappled with the profound grief of losing his mother and the overwhelming responsibility of arranging the funeral, he found it increasingly challenging to effectively communicate with Lucy about his emotional state and the support he needed. Similarly, Lucy, feeling neglected and misunderstood, struggled to express her concerns and desires to Sipho, exacerbating the emotional distance between them.

Their inability to communicate openly and honestly about their needs and emotions left both partners feeling isolated and unheard, further straining their relationship. This breakdown in communication not only affected their ability to navigate through the challenges they were facing but also impacted their sexual intimacy. Without clear and open communication about their sexual desires, boundaries, and concerns, Sipho and Lucy found it difficult to connect on a deeper level and meet each other's needs in the bedroom.

In essence, the story of Sipho and Lucy serves as a reminder of the importance of effective communication in building intimacy and understanding within a relationship. By prioritizing open and honest dialogue about their sexual needs and desires, couples can overcome communication barriers and strengthen their emotional connection, paving the way for a more fulfilling and satisfying sexual relationship.

Effective communication goes beyond mere exchange of words; it encompasses active listening, empathy, and mutual understanding. It involves not only expressing one's thoughts and feelings honestly but also listening attentively to your partner's perspective without judgment or defensiveness. In the case of Sipho and Lucy, effective communication would have entailed Sipho openly expressing his emotional struggles and needs, while Lucy actively listened and offered support without feeling neglected or overlooked.

However, communication alone may not suffice if there is no mutual understanding and empathy. Mutual understanding requires both partners to empathize with each other's experiences, emotions, and needs, even if they may differ from their own. It involves putting oneself in their partner's shoes, acknowledging their perspective, and validating their feelings. In the scenario of Sipho and Lucy, mutual understanding would have enabled Lucy to empathize with Sipho's grief and responsibilities, offering support and understanding instead of feeling neglected.

Moreover, relationships often require sacrifice, where partners may need to prioritize their partner's needs and well-being over their own desires or feelings. In Lucy's case, sacrificing her feelings of neglect and prioritizing Sipho's emotional needs during his time of grief could have strengthened their bond and created a deeper sense of connection. By understanding the responsibilities and emotional strain Sipho was facing, Lucy could have offered unconditional support and empathy, allowing Sipho to grieve without the added pressure of satisfying her emotional needs.

Effective communication in the realm of sexual intimacy on the other hand involves a willingness to explore and discuss one's desires, boundaries, and fantasies openly and without judgment. This requires creating a safe and non-judgmental space where both partners feel comfortable expressing their needs and desires without fear of criticism or rejection. By creating an environment of open communication and vulnerability, couples can deepen their understanding of each other's sexual preferences and enhance their sexual connection.

Additionally, addressing communication breakdowns surrounding sexual intimacy often requires a willingness to seek professional help or couples therapy. A qualified sex therapist can provide guidance and support in navigating difficult conversations about sexual needs and desires, facilitating communication between partners, and exploring strategies to enhance sexual satisfaction and intimacy. Seeking therapy not only allows couples to address underlying issues and barriers to intimacy but also empowers them with tools and techniques to improve their sexual relationship and overall connection.

In conclusion, effective communication and mutual understanding are paramount in nurturing intimacy and connection within a relationship, particularly in the realm of sexual intimacy. By prioritizing open and honest dialogue, empathetic listening, and a willingness to sacrifice for each other's well-being, couples can overcome communication barriers and strengthen their emotional bond. Whether through self-reflection, couples therapy, or seeking professional help, addressing communication breakdowns surrounding sexual intimacy is essential for cultivating a healthy and fulfilling relationship.

Ultimately, by embracing effective communication, mutual understanding, and a commitment to each other's emotional and sexual needs, couples can navigate through challenges, overcome obstacles, and build a strong and resilient foundation for their relationship. Through ongoing communication and mutual support, couples can enhance their sexual connection, deepen their emotional intimacy, and cultivate a relationship that thrives on trust, empathy, and love.

c. Performance Anxiety

Performance anxiety encompasses a range of issues related to sexual performance, including erectile dysfunction, premature ejaculation, or difficulty reaching orgasm. These challenges can profoundly affect both sexual satisfaction and self-esteem, placing strain on the individual and the relationship as a whole. Performance anxiety often arises from a fear of failure or judgment, leading to heightened stress and pressure during sexual encounters.

Anxiety in the context of sexual intimacy refers to feelings of worry, nervousness, or fear that arise before, during, or after sexual encounters. This anxiety can stem from various sources, including past negative experiences, societal expectations, performance pressure, or relationship dynamics. Individuals experiencing sexual anxiety may feel anxious about their ability to perform sexually, satisfy their partner, or meet certain expectations.

The negative effects of sexual anxiety can be far-reaching, impacting both individuals and their relationships. On an individual level, sexual anxiety can lead to a range of physical and psychological symptoms, such as rapid heartbeat, sweating, muscle tension, difficulty concentrating, and intrusive thoughts. These symptoms can significantly interfere with sexual arousal, pleasure, and overall satisfaction, making it challenging to fully engage in intimate experiences.

Moreover, sexual anxiety can take a toll on self-esteem and confidence, causing individuals to doubt their sexual abilities and desirability. This can create a vicious cycle where the fear of sexual performance issues leads to increased anxiety, further exacerbating the problem. Over time, untreated sexual anxiety may contribute to feelings of inadequacy, shame, and frustration, ultimately affecting one's overall well-being and quality of life.

Common Challenges In Sexual Intimacy

In the context of relationships, sexual anxiety can strain intimate connections and erode trust and communication between partners. Individuals experiencing sexual anxiety may avoid sexual encounters altogether or engage in avoidance behaviors to alleviate their anxiety, leading to feelings of rejection or neglect in their partner. This can create tension, resentment, and emotional distance within the relationship, further exacerbating the problem.

Additionally, partners may misinterpret their partner's sexual anxiety as a lack of attraction or interest, leading to misunderstandings and conflict. Over time, unresolved sexual anxiety can erode intimacy and satisfaction in the relationship, diminishing the quality of the sexual bond and overall relationship satisfaction.

Overall, sexual anxiety can have profound implications for both individuals and their relationships, affecting sexual satisfaction, self-esteem, and relationship dynamics. Recognizing the signs of sexual anxiety and seeking support to address underlying issues is essential for nurturing healthy and fulfilling intimate connections.

d. Past Trauma:

Traumatic experiences from the past can significantly impact individuals' experiences of sexual intimacy in the present. Whether stemming from sexual abuse, previous relationships, or adverse childhood experiences, past trauma can cast a long shadow over current intimate interactions, creating challenges and barriers to building healthy relationships.

Individuals who have experienced past trauma may carry emotional scars and unresolved feelings of pain, fear, or shame that can interfere with their ability to engage in intimate relationships. These traumatic experiences can manifest in various ways, including difficulties trusting others, fear of intimacy, low self-esteem, and heightened anxiety or hypervigilance.

In the context of sexual intimacy, past trauma can profoundly affect individuals' feelings of safety, vulnerability, and pleasure during sexual encounters. Survivors of sexual abuse, for example, may struggle with feelings of powerlessness, guilt, or shame surrounding their sexuality, making it challenging to establish healthy boundaries and assert their needs in intimate relationships.

Moreover, past trauma can impact individuals' perceptions of themselves and their bodies, leading to negative body image and self-esteem issues that hinder their ability to fully engage in sexual experiences. Additionally, unresolved trauma may trigger emotional flashbacks or dissociative episodes during intimate moments, further complicating the path to sexual satisfaction and connection.

In relationships, past trauma can create significant challenges, as survivors may struggle to trust and open up to their partners fully. The fear of being re-traumatized or betrayed can lead to emotional distancing, avoidance of intimacy, and difficulty forming secure attachments. This can strain communication, erode trust, and diminish the quality of the relationship over time.

Overall, past trauma can exert a profound influence on individuals' experiences of sexual intimacy, shaping their beliefs, attitudes, and behaviors in intimate relationships. Recognizing the impact of past trauma and seeking support to address and heal from these wounds is essential for nurturing healthy, fulfilling, and mutually satisfying intimate connections.

e. Body Image Concerns:

Negative body image and self-esteem issues can significantly impact individuals' experiences of sexual intimacy, creating barriers that hinder their ability to fully engage and find pleasure in sexual experiences.

Body image concerns often stem from societal standards of beauty, media influence, past experiences of criticism or rejection, and internalized beliefs about one's appearance. Individuals who struggle with negative body image may feel self-conscious, ashamed, or insecure about their physical appearance, leading to feelings of inadequacy and unworthiness in sexual settings.

In the context of sexual intimacy, negative body image can manifest in various ways, including reluctance to undress or be seen naked, avoidance of certain sexual positions or activities, and heightened anxiety or discomfort during intimate moments. These concerns can interfere with individuals' ability to relax, be present, and fully enjoy the experience, ultimately impacting their overall satisfaction and fulfillment in sexual relationships.

Moreover, negative body image can affect individuals' perceptions of their own sexuality and desirability, leading to feelings of inadequacy or reluctance to initiate sexual encounters. This can create tension and communication barriers within relationships, as partners may struggle to understand and address each other's insecurities and concerns.

Addressing body image concerns requires a combination of self-reflection, self-compassion, and open communication with partners. Individuals can work on challenging negative thoughts and beliefs about their bodies, practicing self-care and acceptance, and seeking professional support or therapy when needed.

In relationships, partners can play a supportive role by offering reassurance, validation, and encouragement, creating a safe and accepting environment where individuals feel valued and accepted for who they are. By encouraging open dialogue and understanding, couples can navigate body image concerns together and cultivate a deeper sense of intimacy and connection based on acceptance and mutual respect.

QUESTIONS FREQUENTLY ASKED IN RELATION TO SEXUAL INTIMACY:

1. Am I normal?

Question: Are struggles with orgasm common among women?

Answer: Yes, struggles with orgasm are common among women. Many factors, including physical, psychological, and relational aspects, can contribute to difficulties in achieving orgasm. It's important to recognize that each person's experience with orgasm is unique, and what works for one individual may not necessarily work for another. Seeking support from healthcare professionals or sex therapists can help individuals address and overcome these challenges in a supportive and understanding environment.

Question: Is performance anxiety a normal concern for men?

Answer: Yes, performance anxiety is a common concern for men, especially in sexual situations. It can manifest as difficulty achieving or maintaining an erection (erectile dysfunction), premature ejaculation, or concerns about sexual performance in general. Performance anxiety often stems from fear of judgment, pressure to perform, past negative sexual experiences, or underlying psychological issues. While occasional performance anxiety is normal, persistent or severe anxiety may require professional help from a healthcare provider or therapist to address underlying causes and develop coping strategies.

Question: How often should couples be having sex?

Answer: The frequency of sexual activity that is considered "normal" or healthy for couples can vary greatly depending on individual preferences, desires, and circumstances. There is no one-size-fits-all answer to how often couples should be having sex. Some couples may be content with having sex less frequently, while others may desire more frequent intimacy. Ultimately, what matters most is that both partners feel satisfied and fulfilled in their sexual relationship. Effective communication and mutual understanding are key in navigating sexual frequency and ensuring that both partners' needs are met.

2. Orgasm Struggles

Question: Why am I unable to achieve orgasm?

Answer: Difficulty achieving orgasm can stem from various factors, including physical, psychological, and relational issues. Physical factors may include medical conditions, medications, hormonal imbalances, or changes in anatomy. Psychological factors such as stress, anxiety, depression, past trauma, or negative body image can also contribute to orgasmic difficulties. Additionally, relational issues like communication problems, unresolved conflicts, or lack of emotional connection with a partner can affect orgasmic response. It's essential to explore these factors with a healthcare provider or a mental health professional to identify the underlying cause and find appropriate solutions tailored to individual needs.

Question: Is there something wrong with me if I can't orgasm?

Answer: Experiencing difficulty in achieving orgasm doesn't necessarily mean there's something wrong with you. Orgasmic response varies among individuals, and many factors, both physical and psychological, can influence it. It's essential to remember that sexual experiences are highly individual, and what works for one person may not work for another. If you're concerned about your ability to orgasm, it can be helpful to explore potential underlying factors with a healthcare provider or a mental health professional who can offer support and guidance tailored to your specific needs.

Common Challenges In Sexual Intimacy

Question: How can I achieve orgasm with my partner?

Answer: Achieving orgasm with a partner involves open communication, exploration, and understanding of each other's bodies and desires. Here are some tips that may help:

a. Communicate openly: Discuss your desires, preferences, and any concerns with your partner in a non-judgmental and supportive environment. Open communication can help both partners understand each other's needs better.

b. Explore together: Experiment with different sexual activities, positions, and techniques to discover what feels pleasurable for both partners. Explore erogenous zones and try new things to enhance arousal and satisfaction.

c. Focus on arousal: Take your time to build arousal through foreplay, kissing, touching, and other forms of sensual stimulation. Arousal is an essential component of reaching orgasm for many individuals.

d. Relax and reduce stress: Stress and anxiety can interfere with sexual response and make it difficult to orgasm. Practice relaxation techniques such as deep breathing, mindfulness, or yoga to help calm your mind and body.

e. Use lubrication: Lubrication can reduce friction and discomfort during sexual activity, making it easier to achieve orgasm. Experiment with different types of lubricants to find one that works best for you and your partner.

f. Consider seeking professional help: If you continue to experience difficulty achieving orgasm despite trying different strategies, consider seeking support from a sex therapist or healthcare provider. They can offer guidance, advice, and personalized techniques to help you overcome barriers to orgasm.

Remember that achieving orgasm is not the sole measure of sexual satisfaction or intimacy. Focus on enjoying the journey of exploration and connection with your partner, and be patient and compassionate with yourself along the way.

3. Reviving Intimacy

Question: How can we reignite the passion in our relationship?

Answer: Reigniting passion in a relationship involves intentional effort and a willingness to explore new ways of connecting with your partner. Here are some suggestions to help reignite the passion:

a. Prioritize quality time together: Set aside dedicated time to spend with your partner, free from distractions and obligations. Plan activities that you both enjoy and that promote bonding and intimacy.

b. Communicate openly: Talk to your partner about your desires, fantasies, and what you find exciting in the relationship. Share your thoughts and feelings openly and encourage your partner to do the same.

c. Explore new experiences together: Try new activities, hobbies, or adventures as a couple to keep things fresh and exciting. Whether it's traveling to a new destination, taking a dance class, or trying out a new hobby, shared experiences can reignite passion and create lasting memories.

d. Prioritize physical intimacy: Physical touch and affection are important components of passion in a relationship. Make time for cuddling, kissing, and intimate moments with your partner to nurture the physical connection between you.

e. Keep the romance alive: Surprise your partner with thoughtful gestures, love notes, or small gifts to show them how much you care. Plan romantic dates or special evenings together to keep the romance alive and show your appreciation for each other.

Common Challenges In Sexual Intimacy

f. Invest in your relationship: Relationships require ongoing effort and attention to thrive. Make a commitment to invest in your relationship by attending couples therapy, reading relationship books together, or participating in relationship-building exercises.

Remember that reigniting passion takes time and effort from both partners. Be patient with each other as you navigate this journey together, and focus on building a strong foundation of love, trust, and intimacy in your relationship.

Question: What can we do to increase the frequency of sexual encounters?

Answer: Increasing the frequency of sexual encounters in a relationship requires open communication, mutual understanding, and a willingness to prioritize intimacy. Here are some strategies to help increase sexual frequency:

a. Communicate openly: Talk to your partner about your desires and needs regarding sexual intimacy. Discuss your expectations, preferences, and any obstacles that may be affecting your sexual frequency. Encourage your partner to share their thoughts and feelings as well.

b. Schedule regular "sex dates": Set aside dedicated time in your schedule for sexual intimacy, just like you would for any other important activity. This can help ensure that you prioritize time for connection and intimacy amidst your busy lives.

c. Prioritize self-care: Taking care of yourself physically, mentally, and emotionally can help improve your libido and desire for sexual intimacy. Practice stress management techniques, prioritize sleep, eat a balanced diet, and engage in regular exercise to support your overall well-being.

d. Create a romantic and inviting atmosphere: Set the mood for intimacy by creating a romantic and comfortable environment in your bedroom.

Common Challenges In Sexual Intimacy

Light candles, play soft music, and use sensual scents to enhance the ambiance and make the space inviting for sexual encounters.

e. Experiment with new activities and techniques: Keep things exciting and fresh by trying out new sexual activities, positions, or techniques with your partner. Explore each other's fantasies and desires to keep the sexual spark alive and maintain interest in intimacy.

f. Show affection outside the bedroom: Physical touch and affection throughout the day can help build anticipation and desire for sexual intimacy. Hug, kiss, cuddle, and engage in other forms of non-sexual touch to maintain a connection with your partner.

g. Address any underlying issues: If there are underlying issues such as stress, relationship conflicts, or health concerns that are impacting your sexual frequency, address them together with your partner. Seek professional help if needed to overcome obstacles and improve your sexual relationship.

Remember that every couple's sexual frequency is unique, and there's no "right" or "wrong" amount of sex to have. Focus on finding a balance that works for both you and your partner, and prioritize open communication, mutual satisfaction, and intimacy in your relationship.

Question: Are there strategies for revitalizing our sex life?

Answer: Revitalizing your sex life can breathe new energy and excitement into your relationship. Here are some strategies to help you revitalize your sex life:

a. Communication: Open and honest communication is key. Talk to your partner about your desires, fantasies, and what you both enjoy in the bedroom. Discuss any concerns or challenges you may be facing and work together to find solutions.

b. Try Something New: Break out of your routine and experiment with new activities, positions, or role-playing scenarios. Explore each other's fantasies and be open to trying new things to keep the excitement alive.

c. Set the Mood: Create a romantic and inviting atmosphere in your bedroom. Light candles, play soft music, and use sensual scents to enhance the ambiance and make the space more conducive to intimacy.

d. Prioritize Intimacy: Schedule regular "date nights" or intimate moments with your partner where you can focus solely on each other and reconnect emotionally and physically.

e. Focus on Foreplay: Spend time on foreplay to build anticipation and arousal before engaging in sexual activity. Explore different types of touch, kissing, and caressing to enhance pleasure and intimacy.

f. Invest in Self-Care: Take care of yourself physically, mentally, and emotionally. Engage in activities that make you feel good about yourself and prioritize your overall well-being, which can positively impact your sex life.

g. Address Relationship Issues: Address any underlying relationship issues that may be affecting your sex life. Work on improving communication, resolving conflicts, and strengthening your emotional connection with your partner.

h. Seek Professional Help: If you're struggling to revitalize your sex life on your own, consider seeking guidance from a sex therapist or counselor. They can provide personalized advice and techniques to help you overcome challenges and enhance your sexual relationship.

Remember that revitalizing your sex life is a journey that requires effort and commitment from both partners. Stay open-minded, adventurous, and willing to explore new possibilities together to keep the passion alive in your relationship.

4. Communication Challenges

Question: How do we effectively communicate about our sexual needs?

Answer: Effectively communicating about your sexual needs is crucial for maintaining a healthy and satisfying sexual relationship. Here are some tips to help you communicate effectively with your partner about your sexual needs:

a. Create a Safe Space: Choose a time and place where you both feel comfortable and relaxed to have an open and honest conversation about your sexual needs. Ensure that you won't be interrupted and that you have each other's full attention.

b. Use "I" Statements: Express your feelings, desires, and concerns using "I" statements to take ownership of your own experiences. For example, say "I feel..." or "I would like..." instead of placing blame or making accusations.

c. Be Specific: Clearly articulate your sexual needs, preferences, and boundaries to your partner. Be specific about what you enjoy and what you would like to explore together. Avoid making assumptions and encourage your partner to do the same.

d. Listen Actively: Practice active listening by giving your partner your full attention without interrupting or judging. Show empathy and understanding by acknowledging their perspective and validating their feelings.

e. Encourage Feedback: Invite your partner to share their thoughts, feelings, and desires openly and honestly. Encourage them to provide feedback on what they enjoy and what they would like to try differently.

f. Be Respectful: Respect your partner's boundaries, preferences, and comfort levels at all times. Avoid pressuring or coercing them into activities they are not comfortable with and be mindful of their feelings and reactions.

g. Stay Open-Minded: Approach the conversation with an open mind and a willingness to explore new ideas and experiences. Be receptive to your partner's suggestions and be willing to compromise to find common ground.

h. Practice Empathy: Put yourself in your partner's shoes and try to understand their perspective, feelings, and needs. Show empathy and compassion towards their experiences and be supportive of their desires.

i. Follow Up: Check in with each other regularly to ensure that your sexual needs are being met and that you're both satisfied with the direction your sexual relationship is taking. Be willing to revisit the conversation as needed and make adjustments as necessary.

By following these tips and practicing open and honest communication, you can effectively communicate about your sexual needs with your partner and nurture a deeper connection and greater satisfaction in your sexual relationship.

Question: What are some ways to introduce sensitive topics related to sex?

Answer: Introducing sensitive topics related to sex can be challenging, but it's essential for creating open communication and addressing issues in your sexual relationship. Here are some ways to approach these conversations:

a. Choose the Right Time and Place: Pick a time when both you and your partner are relaxed and not distracted. Find a private space where you can have a conversation without interruptions.

Common Challenges In Sexual Intimacy

b. Use Gentle Language: Approach the topic with sensitivity and care, using gentle language to express yourself. Avoid using accusatory or judgmental language that may put your partner on the defensive.

c. Express Your Feelings: Share your thoughts and emotions openly and honestly, using "I" statements to take ownership of your feelings. For example, say "I feel worried about..." or "I would like to talk about..."

d. Start with Positive Feedback: Begin the conversation by acknowledging the positive aspects of your relationship and expressing appreciation for your partner. This can help set a positive tone for the discussion.

e. Be Direct but Tactful: Be direct in expressing your concerns or desires, but do so in a tactful and respectful manner. Avoid beating around the bush or hinting at what you want to discuss.

f. Listen Actively: Give your partner the opportunity to share their perspective and listen to their thoughts and feelings without interrupting or judging. Show empathy and understanding towards their experiences.

g. Focus on Solutions: Instead of dwelling on the problem, focus on finding solutions together. Brainstorm ideas and strategies for addressing the issue and improving your sexual relationship.

h. Seek Consent: Respect your partner's boundaries and seek their consent before discussing sensitive topics. Make sure they feel comfortable and willing to engage in the conversation.

i. Be Patient and Understanding: Be patient and understanding if your partner needs time to process the information or express themselves. Give them the space and support they need to share their thoughts and feelings.

j. Follow Up: Check in with your partner after the conversation to see how they're feeling and whether any further discussion or action is needed. Continue to communicate openly and honestly to maintain a healthy sexual relationship.

By approaching sensitive topics related to sex with empathy, understanding, and respect, you can nurture open communication with your partner and strengthen your sexual relationship.

Question: How can we create a safe space for discussing sexual concerns?

Answer: Creating a safe space for discussing sexual concerns is crucial for building open communication and addressing issues in your sexual relationship. Here are some tips for creating a safe environment:

a. Establish Trust: Build trust with your partner by demonstrating reliability, honesty, and respect in your relationship. Trust lays the foundation for open communication and encourages vulnerability.

b. Choose the Right Time: Pick a time when both you and your partner are relaxed and not distracted. Avoid bringing up sensitive topics during times of stress or conflict.

c. Find a Private Setting: Select a private space where you can have an open and honest conversation without interruptions or distractions. This allows both partners to feel comfortable expressing themselves freely.

d. Listen Without Judgment: Practice active listening by focusing on your partner's words without interrupting or judging. Show empathy and understanding towards their experiences, even if they differ from your own.

e. Use "I" Statements: Express your thoughts and feelings using "I" statements to take ownership of your emotions. For example, say "I feel concerned about..." or "I would like to discuss..."

f. Encourage Openness: Encourage your partner to express themselves openly and honestly without fear of judgment or criticism. Assure them that their feelings and concerns are valid and respected.

Common Challenges In Sexual Intimacy

g. Respect Boundaries: Respect your partner's boundaries and comfort levels during the conversation. Avoid pressuring them to discuss topics they're not ready to address and seek their consent before delving into sensitive issues.

h. Validate Feelings: Validate your partner's feelings and experiences by acknowledging their emotions and offering empathy and support. Let them know that you understand and care about their concerns.

i. Focus on Solutions: Instead of dwelling on the problem, focus on finding solutions together. Collaborate with your partner to brainstorm ideas and strategies for addressing the issue and improving your sexual relationship.

j. Follow Up: Check in with your partner after the conversation to see how they're feeling and whether any further discussion or action is needed. Continue to communicate openly and honestly to maintain a safe and supportive environment for discussing sexual concerns.

By implementing these strategies, you can create a safe and supportive space for discussing sexual concerns with your partner, nurturing open communication, and strengthening your sexual relationship.

5. Performance Anxiety and Dysfunction

Question: Why am I experiencing performance issues?

Answer: Experiencing performance issues can be concerning, but it's essential to remember that they are relatively common and often have underlying causes that can be addressed. Here are some potential reasons why you might be experiencing performance issues:

1. Physical Factors: Performance issues such as erectile dysfunction or premature ejaculation can sometimes be attributed to physical factors such as underlying health conditions (e.g., diabetes, heart disease, high

Common Challenges In Sexual Intimacy

blood pressure), medication side effects, hormonal imbalances, or neurological disorders.

b. Psychological Factors: Stress, anxiety, depression, and other mental health issues can significantly impact sexual performance. Performance anxiety, in particular, can create a cycle of worry and self-doubt that interferes with sexual function.

c. Relationship Issues: Conflict, unresolved issues, or communication problems within your relationship can affect your ability to perform sexually. Feelings of resentment, anger, or disconnect from your partner may contribute to performance issues.

d. Self-esteem and Body Image: Negative self-image, low self-esteem, or body image concerns can undermine confidence and sexual performance. Feeling insecure about your appearance or abilities may lead to anxiety and self-doubt in sexual situations.

e. Lifestyle Factors: Unhealthy lifestyle habits such as smoking, excessive alcohol consumption, drug use, lack of exercise, poor diet, and inadequate sleep can impact sexual function and performance. These factors can affect circulation, hormone levels, and overall health, all of which play a role in sexual performance.

f. Performance Pressure: Feeling pressure to perform sexually, whether due to societal expectations, personal beliefs, or perceived standards, can create stress and anxiety that interferes with sexual function. It's essential to approach sex with your partner in a relaxed and comfortable manner, focusing on pleasure rather than performance.

If you're experiencing performance issues, it's crucial to communicate openly with your partner and consider seeking support from a healthcare professional. A doctor or therapist can help identify any underlying physical or psychological factors contributing to the issue and develop a personalized treatment plan to address them. Additionally, practicing stress-reduction techniques, maintaining a healthy lifestyle, and promoting open communication and intimacy with your partner can also support sexual health and performance.

Question: What can I do to overcome performance anxiety?

Answer: Overcoming performance anxiety can be a gradual process, but there are several strategies you can try to manage and reduce it:

a. Education and Understanding: Learn about sexual anatomy, responses, and common myths surrounding sex. Understanding that performance anxiety is common and often temporary can help alleviate some of the pressure.

b. Communication: Openly discuss your concerns and feelings with your partner. Sharing your anxieties can reduce their impact and create a supportive environment.

c. Relaxation Techniques: Practice relaxation techniques such as deep breathing, meditation, or progressive muscle relaxation to calm your mind and body before sexual activity.

d. Focus on Sensations: Instead of fixating on performance or orgasm, focus on the sensations and pleasure of the moment. Mindfulness techniques can help you stay present and enjoy the experience without pressure.

e. Setting Realistic Expectations: Challenge unrealistic expectations about sex and performance. Recognize that sex is not always perfect and that both partners may have varying levels of desire and arousal.

f. Take Things Slow: Take your time with foreplay and intimacy. Slow down and enjoy each other's company without rushing to the end goal of intercourse.

g. Experiment and Explore: Try new activities, positions, or techniques with your partner. Exploring together can add excitement and reduce pressure to perform.

h. Seek Professional Help: If performance anxiety persists or significantly impacts your well-being, consider seeking help from a therapist or counselor who specializes in sexual health. They can provide strategies, support, and guidance tailored to your individual needs.

Remember that overcoming performance anxiety is a process, and it's okay to seek help if you need it. With patience, understanding, and support, you can learn to manage anxiety and enjoy fulfilling sexual experiences.

Question: Are there treatments available for sexual dysfunction?

Answer: Yes, there are various treatments available for sexual dysfunction, depending on the underlying cause. Some common treatments include:

a. Medications: For conditions such as erectile dysfunction or premature ejaculation, medications like Viagra, Cialis, or SSRIs (selective serotonin reuptake inhibitors) may be prescribed by a healthcare professional.

b. Therapy: Counseling or therapy, including cognitive-behavioral therapy (CBT) or sex therapy, can help address psychological factors contributing to sexual dysfunction, such as anxiety, depression, or past trauma.

c. Hormone Therapy: Hormonal imbalances, such as low testosterone levels in men or hormonal fluctuations in women, can contribute to sexual dysfunction. Hormone replacement therapy may be recommended to address these issues.

d. Lifestyle Changes: Making healthy lifestyle changes, such as maintaining a balanced diet, exercising regularly, reducing stress, getting enough sleep, and avoiding alcohol and substance abuse, can improve overall sexual health.

e. Devices and Aids: Devices such as vacuum erection devices or penile implants may be recommended for men with erectile dysfunction. Additionally, lubricants, vibrators, or other sexual aids may help enhance sexual function and pleasure.

f. Surgery: In some cases, surgical procedures may be necessary to address physical causes of sexual dysfunction, such as Peyronie's disease or vaginal prolapse.

g. Alternative Therapies: Alternative treatments like acupuncture, herbal supplements, or pelvic floor exercises (Kegels) may be considered, although their effectiveness varies and should be discussed with a healthcare provider.

It's essential to consult with a healthcare professional, such as a urologist, gynecologist, or sex therapist, to determine the most appropriate treatment plan based on individual needs and circumstances. They can provide personalized recommendations and support to help address sexual dysfunction and improve overall sexual health and well-being.

6. Healing and Trust

Question: How can we heal from past sexual traumas?

Answer: Healing from past sexual traumas can be a complex and challenging process, but it is possible with patience, self-compassion, and support. Here are some steps that may help:

a. Seek Therapy: Consider seeking therapy with a qualified mental health professional, such as a therapist specializing in trauma or sexual abuse. Therapy can provide a safe space to process emotions, gain insight into how past traumas are affecting your life, and learn coping strategies to manage symptoms.

b. Practice Self-Care: Engage in self-care activities that promote relaxation, stress reduction, and overall well-being. This may include mindfulness practices, exercise, spending time in nature, creative outlets, or nurturing relationships with supportive friends and family members.

c. Educate Yourself: Educate yourself about trauma and its effects on the mind and body. Understanding how trauma impacts thoughts, emotions, and behaviors can help you make sense of your experiences and develop a sense of empowerment in your healing journey.

d. Set Boundaries: Establish healthy boundaries in your relationships and prioritize your own needs and safety. Learn to recognize and assertively communicate your boundaries, and surround yourself with people who respect and support them.

e. Explore Healing Modalities: Explore different healing modalities that resonate with you, such as somatic experiencing, EMDR (Eye Movement Desensitization and Reprocessing), art therapy, yoga, or meditation. These practices can help release stored trauma from the body and promote healing on a physical, emotional, and spiritual level.

f. Connect with Supportive Communities: Connect with support groups or online communities of survivors who have experienced similar traumas. Sharing experiences and resources with others who understand can provide validation, encouragement, and a sense of belonging.

g. Practice Self-Compassion: Be gentle and compassionate with yourself throughout the healing process. Recognize that healing takes time and may involve setbacks or difficult emotions. Treat yourself with kindness, patience, and understanding as you navigate your journey toward healing and recovery.

It's essential to remember that healing from past sexual traumas is a unique and individual process, and there is no one-size-fits-all approach. Be patient with yourself and trust your instincts as you take steps toward healing and reclaiming your sense of safety, autonomy, and empowerment. If you're struggling, don't hesitate to reach out for professional help and support. You deserve healing, and you are not alone in your journey.

Question: What steps can we take to rebuild trust in our relationship?

Answer: Rebuilding trust in a relationship after it has been damaged can be a challenging but achievable process. Here are some steps you can take:

a. Open Communication: Establish open and honest communication with your partner. Both partners should feel safe to express their feelings, concerns, and needs without fear of judgment or retaliation. Make time to listen actively to each other and validate each other's experiences.

b. Transparency: Be transparent and accountable in your actions. Share information openly with your partner and avoid keeping secrets or withholding important details. Building trust requires honesty and integrity in all aspects of the relationship.

c. Consistency: Demonstrate consistent behavior over time to show your commitment to rebuilding trust. Follow through on your promises, be reliable, and show that you can be counted on to support your partner and prioritize the relationship.

d. Apologize and Take Responsibility: If you have caused harm or betrayed your partner's trust, take responsibility for your actions and offer a sincere apology. Acknowledge the hurt you have caused, express genuine remorse, and demonstrate your commitment to making amends.

e. Set Boundaries: Establish clear boundaries and agreements within the relationship to prevent future breaches of trust. Discuss expectations regarding fidelity, honesty, and communication, and mutually agree on guidelines for behavior moving forward.

f. Forgiveness: Practice forgiveness, both for yourself and your partner. Let go of resentment and bitterness, and focus on moving forward together with a clean slate. Forgiveness does not mean forgetting or condoning hurtful behavior but rather releasing the emotional burden and allowing space for healing.

g. Seek Counseling: Consider seeking couples therapy or counseling to navigate the process of rebuilding trust with the guidance of a trained professional. A therapist can provide support, facilitate productive communication, and offer strategies to address underlying issues and rebuild intimacy.

h. Patience and Time: Rebuilding trust takes time and patience. Be realistic about the timeline for rebuilding trust and understand that it may not happen overnight. Be patient with yourself and your partner as you navigate the ups and downs of the healing process.

i. Focus on the Positive: Cultivate a positive and nurturing environment within the relationship. Celebrate progress and small victories along the way, and focus on building new, positive experiences together that strengthen your connection and reinforce trust.

j. Commitment to Growth: Commit to personal and relational growth as individuals and as a couple. Use the challenges you face as opportunities for learning and growth, and be willing to put in the effort and work together to create a healthier, more resilient relationship.

Remember that rebuilding trust is a gradual and ongoing process that requires dedication, effort, and mutual commitment from both partners. With patience, communication, and a willingness to heal, it is possible to rebuild trust and create a stronger, more resilient relationship.

7. Enhancing Connection

Question: How do we deepen the emotional connection in our relationship?

Common Challenges In Sexual Intimacy

Answer: Deepening the emotional connection in a relationship is essential for building intimacy, trust, and mutual understanding. Here are some strategies to help you deepen your emotional connection:

a. Open Communication: Nurture open and honest communication with your partner. Share your thoughts, feelings, and experiences openly, and encourage your partner to do the same. Make time for regular check-ins to discuss your relationship, goals, and any concerns or challenges you may be facing.

b. Active Listening: Practice active listening when your partner is speaking. Give them your full attention, maintain eye contact, and show empathy and understanding. Reflect back what they say to ensure you understand their perspective and validate their feelings.

c. Empathy and Understanding: Cultivate empathy and understanding towards your partner's experiences, emotions, and needs. Put yourself in their shoes and strive to see things from their perspective. Validate their feelings and demonstrate compassion and support, even when you may not fully agree.

d. Quality Time Together: Make time for regular quality time together to nurture your emotional connection. Engage in activities you both enjoy, such as shared hobbies, meaningful conversations, or intimate moments of connection. Prioritize spending uninterrupted time together to strengthen your bond.

e. Express Appreciation and Affection: Show your partner appreciation and affection regularly. Express gratitude for their presence in your life, acknowledge their efforts and contributions, and express love and affection through words, gestures, and physical touch.

f. Shared Goals and Values: Identify and pursue shared goals, values, and interests that strengthen your connection as a couple. Collaborate on projects, adventures, or personal growth pursuits that align with your shared vision for the future and adopt a sense of partnership and unity.

g. Celebrate Milestones and Achievements: Celebrate milestones, achievements, and special moments together as a couple. Acknowledge and celebrate each other's successes, milestones, and accomplishments, and show support and encouragement in pursuing your individual and shared goals.

h. Manage Conflict Constructively: Handle conflicts and disagreements in a constructive and respectful manner. Use healthy communication techniques such as active listening, "I" statements, and compromise to address differences and find mutually satisfactory solutions. Approach conflicts as opportunities for growth and learning rather than sources of division.

i. Practice Vulnerability: Be willing to be vulnerable with your partner and share your innermost thoughts, fears, and insecurities. Allow yourself to be seen and understood authentically, and create a safe space where your partner can do the same. Vulnerability nurtures intimacy and deepens emotional connection.

j. Seek Couples Therapy: Consider seeking couples therapy or counseling to deepen your emotional connection with the guidance of a trained professional. A therapist can provide support, facilitate deeper communication, and offer strategies to address underlying issues and strengthen your bond as a couple.

By incorporating these strategies into your relationship, you can deepen your emotional connection with your partner and create a stronger, more fulfilling bond built on trust, understanding, and love.

Question: What strategies can we use to encourage intimacy outside of the bedroom?

Answer: Encouraging intimacy outside of the bedroom is crucial for strengthening emotional connection and building a deeper bond with your partner. Here are some strategies you can use to cultivate intimacy in various aspects of your relationship:

a. Engage in Meaningful Conversations: Take time to have meaningful conversations with your partner about your thoughts, feelings, dreams, and aspirations. Ask open-ended questions, actively listen to their responses, and share your own thoughts and experiences. This allows you to connect on a deeper level and understand each other better.

b. Quality Time Together: Prioritize spending quality time together doing activities you both enjoy. This could include going for walks, cooking together, exploring new places, or simply cuddling on the couch while watching a movie. The key is to focus on each other and enjoy each other's company without distractions.

c. Show Affection: Express affection towards your partner through small gestures of love and appreciation. This could be holding hands, giving hugs and kisses, or leaving love notes for each other. Physical touch and acts of affection help reinforce your emotional connection and show your partner that you care.

d. Share New Experiences: Explore new experiences together to create lasting memories and deepen your bond. This could involve trying new hobbies, taking classes together, or going on adventures such as hiking, traveling, or camping. Sharing new experiences creates a sense of excitement and connection between partners.

e. Practice Gratitude: Regularly express gratitude for your partner and the things they do for you. Acknowledge their efforts, strengths, and positive qualities, and let them know how much you appreciate them. Gratitude strengthens your connection and reinforces feelings of love and appreciation.

f. Support Each Other's Goals: Show support for your partner's goals, aspirations, and dreams. Encourage them to pursue their passions and be there for them during both the successes and challenges they encounter along the way. Supporting each other's goals strengthens your bond and nurtures a sense of partnership.

g. Engage in Acts of Service: Show love and care for your partner through acts of service that make their life easier or more enjoyable. This could involve helping with household chores, running errands for them, or surprising them with thoughtful gestures. Acts of service demonstrate your commitment to their well-being and strengthen your emotional connection.

h. Share Vulnerability: Be willing to be vulnerable with your partner and share your innermost thoughts, fears, and insecurities. Allow yourself to be seen authentically, and create a safe space where your partner can do the same. Sharing vulnerability builds intimacy and deepens emotional connection.

i. Laugh Together: Don't underestimate the power of laughter in strengthening your bond with your partner. Find opportunities to share jokes, watch comedies together, or reminisce about funny memories. Laughter helps relieve stress, promotes bonding, and brings joy to your relationship.

j. Practice Active Listening: Listen attentively to your partner's thoughts, feelings, and concerns without judgment or interruption. Show empathy and understanding, and validate their experiences and emotions. Active listening creates deeper connection and strengthens trust between partners.

By incorporating these strategies into your relationship, you can build intimacy outside of the bedroom and a stronger, more fulfilling connection with your partner.

Question: Are there activities or exercises that can strengthen our bond as a couple?

Answer: Engaging in activities or exercises together as a couple is an excellent way to strengthen your bond and deepen your connection. Here are some activities and exercises that can help strengthen your relationship:

a. Cooking or Baking Together: Prepare a meal or bake something delicious together. Working as a team in the kitchen creates cooperation, communication, and creativity. Plus, you get to enjoy a tasty treat together afterward!

b. Outdoor Adventures: Go on outdoor adventures such as hiking, biking, camping, or kayaking. Spending time in nature together allows you to unplug from technology, enjoy each other's company, and create lasting memories.

c. Art or Craft Projects: Get creative together by engaging in art or craft projects. Whether it's painting, pottery, scrapbooking, or DIY home decor, working on artistic endeavors together encourages self-expression and collaboration.

d. Dance Classes: Take dance lessons together, whether it's salsa, ballroom, or hip-hop. Dancing promotes physical closeness, coordination, and spontaneity, while also being a fun way to bond and stay active.

e. Volunteer Work: Volunteer for a cause or organization that you both care about. Giving back to the community as a couple creates a sense of purpose, strengthens your bond, and allows you to make a positive impact together.

f. Traveling Together: Plan a getaway or vacation together to explore new destinations and create shared experiences. Traveling allows you to step outside of your comfort zone, learn about different cultures, and build memories that will last a lifetime.

g. Couples' Retreats or Workshops: Attend couples' retreats or workshops focused on relationship building and personal growth. These retreats offer opportunities for reflection, communication, and learning new skills to enhance your relationship.

h. Journaling Together: Start a couple's journal where you can write down your thoughts, feelings, and experiences together. Writing prompts or reflection exercises can help you deepen your connection and understand each other better.

i. Relationship Check-Ins: Schedule regular relationship check-ins where you can discuss your relationship goals, challenges, and dreams for the future. These check-ins promote open communication, strengthen your bond, and ensure that you're both on the same page.

By engaging in these activities and exercises together, you can strengthen your bond as a couple, deepen your connection, and create a more fulfilling and resilient relationship.

8. Body Image and Self-Esteem

Question: How can we overcome negative body image issues in the context of intimacy?

Answer: Overcoming negative body image issues in the context of intimacy requires patience, compassion, and a commitment to self-love and acceptance. Here are some strategies to help you overcome negative body image issues:

a. Practice Self-Compassion: Be kind and gentle with yourself. Practice self-compassion by treating yourself with the same kindness and understanding that you would offer to a friend. Remind yourself that your worth is not defined by your appearance.

Common Challenges In Sexual Intimacy

b. Challenge Negative Thoughts: Challenge negative thoughts about your body by questioning their validity. Replace negative self-talk with positive affirmations and focus on your strengths and qualities beyond physical appearance.

c. Focus on Health, Not Appearance: Shift your focus from achieving a certain body type to prioritizing your overall health and well-being. Engage in activities that make you feel strong, energized, and confident, such as regular exercise, nutritious eating, and adequate sleep.

d. Practice Mindfulness: Cultivate mindfulness by staying present in the moment and practicing acceptance of your body as it is. Engage in mindfulness activities such as deep breathing, meditation, or body scans to create a greater sense of body awareness and acceptance.

e. Explore Sensual and Pleasurable Activities: Focus on sensual and pleasurable activities that allow you to connect with your partner without placing emphasis on physical appearance. Engage in activities such as massage, cuddling, or intimate conversations to nurture intimacy and connection.

f. Communicate with Your Partner: Openly communicate with your partner about your insecurities and concerns regarding body image. Share your feelings and needs, and ask for their support and reassurance. A supportive partner can help you feel accepted and loved for who you are.

g. Challenge Unrealistic Beauty Standards: Recognize that the media often promotes unrealistic beauty standards that can contribute to negative body image. Challenge these standards by seeking out diverse representations of beauty and surrounding yourself with body-positive influences.

h. Seek Professional Support: Consider seeking support from a therapist or counselor who specializes in body image issues or sexual health.

Therapy can provide you with coping strategies, tools for self-compassion, and a safe space to explore and process your feelings.

i. Engage in Body-Positive Practices: Surround yourself with body-positive messages and communities that celebrate diversity and promote self-love. Follow body-positive influencers on social media, read books or articles about body acceptance, and engage in activities that uplift and empower you.

j. Celebrate Your Body: Practice gratitude for your body and all that it allows you to do. Celebrate your body's strength, resilience, and uniqueness. Engage in activities that make you feel confident and empowered, whether it's dancing, wearing clothing that makes you feel good, or expressing yourself creatively.

By implementing these strategies and embracing a mindset of self-love and acceptance, you can overcome negative body image issues and cultivate a more positive and fulfilling relationship with yourself and your partner.

Question: What role does self-esteem play in sexual satisfaction?

Answer: Self-esteem plays a crucial role in sexual satisfaction as it influences how individuals perceive themselves and their worthiness of love, pleasure, and intimacy. Here's how self-esteem impacts sexual satisfaction:

a. Confidence and Assertiveness: Individuals with high self-esteem are more likely to feel confident in expressing their desires, boundaries, and preferences in sexual encounters. They are assertive in communicating their needs and advocating for their pleasure, leading to more fulfilling sexual experiences.

b. Body Image: Self-esteem affects how individuals perceive their bodies and physical appearance. Those with positive self-esteem are more likely to have a positive body image, which enhances their comfort and confidence in their own skin during sexual activities. Conversely, individuals with low self-esteem may experience body-related insecurities that hinder their ability to fully engage in sexual intimacy.

c. Emotional Vulnerability: Self-esteem influences one's ability to be emotionally vulnerable and authentic with their partner during intimate moments. Individuals with high self-esteem are more likely to trust their partner, express vulnerability, and experience emotional intimacy, which enhances sexual satisfaction. Conversely, low self-esteem may lead to emotional barriers and difficulties in connecting deeply with a partner, impacting sexual satisfaction.

d. Sexual Assertiveness: Individuals with high self-esteem are more likely to assert their sexual desires, preferences, and boundaries, leading to a more mutually satisfying sexual experience. They feel empowered to communicate their needs and advocate for their pleasure, which nurtures a sense of empowerment and satisfaction in sexual encounters.

e. Relationship Satisfaction: Self-esteem also influences overall relationship satisfaction, which in turn affects sexual satisfaction. Individuals with high self-esteem tend to have healthier, more fulfilling relationships characterized by trust, respect, and intimacy, which positively impact sexual satisfaction. Conversely, low self-esteem may contribute to relationship insecurity, conflict, and dissatisfaction, which can detract from sexual fulfillment.

f. Self-Worth and Pleasure: High self-esteem is associated with a greater sense of self-worth and deservingness of pleasure and satisfaction in sexual relationships. Individuals with positive self-esteem are more likely to prioritize their own pleasure and prioritize their needs in sexual encounters, leading to increased sexual satisfaction.

Overall, self-esteem plays a multifaceted role in sexual satisfaction, influencing confidence, body image, emotional intimacy, assertiveness, relationship dynamics, and self-worth. Cultivating positive self-esteem through self-care, self-compassion, and healthy relationship dynamics can enhance sexual satisfaction and overall well-being.

Question: Are there techniques for improving body confidence during sexual encounters?

Answer: There are several techniques individuals can employ to improve body confidence during sexual encounters:

a. Practice Self-Compassion: Treat yourself with kindness and understanding, especially when it comes to body image. Recognize that everyone has insecurities and imperfections, and practice self-compassion by speaking to yourself in a supportive and understanding manner.

b. Challenge Negative Thoughts: Challenge negative thoughts and beliefs about your body by focusing on its strengths and capabilities rather than perceived flaws. Reframe negative self-talk into more positive and realistic affirmations that promote self-acceptance and appreciation.

c. Focus on Sensations: During sexual encounters, shift your focus away from how your body looks and towards the physical sensations and pleasure you're experiencing. By immersing yourself in the moment and focusing on the sensations of touch, pleasure, and connection, you can enhance your enjoyment of the experience regardless of body insecurities.

d. Experiment with Lighting and Setting: Create a comfortable and inviting environment for sexual intimacy by experimenting with lighting and setting. Dimming the lights or using candles can help create a soft, flattering ambiance that minimizes self-consciousness and enhances relaxation and arousal.

e. Communicate with Your Partner: Openly communicate with your partner about your body image concerns and insecurities. Share your feelings and fears in a non-judgmental and supportive manner, and discuss ways in which your partner can help you feel more comfortable and confident during sexual encounters.

f. Explore Sensual Touch: Engage in sensual activities that focus on touch and intimacy, such as sensual massage or cuddling. These activities can help you feel more connected to your partner and your own body, nurturing a sense of acceptance and appreciation for your physical self.

g. Practice Mindfulness: Incorporate mindfulness techniques into your daily routine to cultivate present-moment awareness and self-acceptance. Mindfulness practices such as meditation, deep breathing, or body scans can help you become more attuned to your body's sensations and less focused on negative thoughts about your appearance.

h. Seek Professional Support: If body image concerns significantly impact your well-being and sexual satisfaction, consider seeking support from a therapist or counselor who specializes in body image issues or sexual health. Therapy can provide you with coping strategies, tools, and support to address underlying insecurities and improve body confidence.

By incorporating these techniques into your life, you can gradually enhance your body confidence and feel more comfortable and empowered in your own skin during sexual encounters. Remember that building body confidence is a journey, and it's okay to seek support and take small steps towards greater self-acceptance and appreciation.

9. Exploring Fantasies and New Activities

Question: How do we safely explore sexual fantasies with each other?

Answer: Exploring sexual fantasies with your partner can be an exciting and intimate experience, but it's essential to approach it with care and communication to ensure both partners feel safe and comfortable. Here are some steps to safely explore sexual fantasies together:

Common Challenges In Sexual Intimacy

a. Open and Honest Communication: Start by having an open and honest conversation with your partner about your sexual desires, interests, and boundaries. Create a safe and non-judgmental space where you can both share your fantasies without fear of criticism or rejection.

b. Establish Trust: Trust is crucial when exploring sexual fantasies. Make sure you both feel emotionally secure and trust each other to respect boundaries and prioritize each other's comfort and well-being.

c. Set Boundaries: Discuss and establish clear boundaries before delving into any sexual fantasies. Talk about what you're comfortable with and what you're not, and be respectful of each other's limits. Agree on a safe word or signal that either partner can use to stop or pause the activity if they feel uncomfortable.

d. Start Slowly: Begin by exploring fantasies in a gradual and incremental manner. Start with fantasies that feel less intimidating or intense and gradually work your way up to more adventurous scenarios as you both become more comfortable and trusting with each other.

e. Use Fantasy Props or Role-Play: Incorporate fantasy props or engage in role-playing to add excitement and realism to your exploration. Experiment with costumes, toys, or scenarios that align with your fantasies and enhance the experience for both partners.

f. Respect Each Other's Limits: Respect each other's boundaries and limits throughout the exploration process. If either partner expresses discomfort or reluctance, be understanding and supportive, and refrain from pressuring or coercing them into activities they're not comfortable with.

g. Check-In Regularly: Check in with each other regularly during and after exploring sexual fantasies to ensure both partners feel safe, comfortable, and satisfied with the experience. Discuss what worked well, what didn't, and how you can improve or adjust for future explorations.

Common Challenges In Sexual Intimacy

h. Seek Consent: Always seek explicit consent from your partner before engaging in any sexual activity, including exploring fantasies. Consent should be enthusiastic, ongoing, and freely given by all parties involved.

i. Respect Privacy: Respect each other's privacy and confidentiality when discussing or acting out sexual fantasies. Keep intimate details and experiences between the two of you and refrain from sharing them with others without explicit consent.

j. Seek Professional Help if Needed: If exploring sexual fantasies triggers emotional distress or relationship issues, consider seeking guidance from a qualified therapist or counselor who specializes in sexual health and relationship dynamics.

By following these steps and prioritizing open communication, trust, and mutual respect, you can safely and enjoyably explore sexual fantasies with your partner, deepening your connection and enhancing your sexual satisfaction together.

Question: What are some new activities we can try to spice up our sex life?

Answer: Spicing up your sex life can be an exciting way to add novelty and passion to your relationship. Here are some new activities you can try to enhance your sexual experiences together:

a. Experiment with Sensory Play: Explore different sensory experiences such as blindfolding, using feathers, ice cubes, or silk scarves to heighten sensations and arousal during foreplay and sex.

b. Introduce Sex Toys: Incorporate sex toys such as vibrators, dildos, or couples' toys into your play to add variety and intensity to your sexual encounters. Experiment with different types of toys and find what works best for both of you.

c. Try New Positions: Explore a variety of sexual positions to discover what feels most pleasurable and stimulating for both partners. Experiment with positions from the Kama Sutra or try variations of classic positions to keep things fresh and exciting.

d. Role-Playing: Engage in role-playing scenarios where you and your partner take on different characters or personas to act out fantasies and explore new dynamics in the bedroom.

e. Erotic Massage: Treat each other to sensual and erotic massages using massage oils or candles to create a relaxing and intimate atmosphere. Take turns massaging each other's bodies, paying attention to erogenous zones and areas of tension.

f. Try New Locations: Break out of the bedroom and explore new locations for sexual encounters, such as the shower, kitchen, living room, or outdoors. Experimenting with different settings can add excitement and novelty to your sex life.

g. Engage in Mutual Masturbation: Masturbate together while watching each other or pleasuring yourselves side by side. Mutual masturbation can be an intimate and arousing way to explore each other's bodies and sexual responses.

h. Role Reversal: Switch up traditional gender roles and take turns initiating sex, taking the lead, or exploring dominant and submissive dynamics in the bedroom.

i. Fantasy Sharing: Share your sexual fantasies with each other and explore ways to incorporate them into your play. Discuss boundaries and consent beforehand to ensure both partners feel comfortable and respected.

Remember to communicate openly with your partner about your desires, boundaries, and preferences, and prioritize mutual pleasure and satisfaction in all your sexual experiences. By trying new activities and

Common Challenges In Sexual Intimacy

staying adventurous, you can keep the spark alive and deepen your connection with each other.

Question: Are there guidelines for introducing new elements into our sexual relationship?

Answer: Introducing new elements into your sexual relationship can be an exciting way to explore new avenues of pleasure and intimacy with your partner. Here are some guidelines to consider when incorporating new elements into your sexual relationship:

a. Open Communication: Start by having an open and honest conversation with your partner about your desires, fantasies, and boundaries. Share your ideas and listen to your partner's thoughts and feelings without judgment. Effective communication is essential for ensuring that both partners feel comfortable and respected throughout the process.

b. Mutual Consent: Prioritize mutual consent and agreement when introducing new elements into your sexual relationship. Both partners should enthusiastically consent to any new activities or experiences and have the freedom to express their boundaries or concerns without pressure.

c. Take It Slow: Introduce new elements gradually and at a pace that feels comfortable for both partners. Rushing into unfamiliar territory can lead to discomfort or resistance. Start with small changes or experiments and gradually build upon them as you both feel more confident and comfortable.

d. Educate Yourselves: Take the time to educate yourselves about the new elements you're interested in exploring. Whether it's trying out new sexual positions, experimenting with **BDSM** (Bondage and Discipline, Dominance and Submission, and Sadism and Masochism), or incorporating sex toys, research the topic together, and discuss any concerns or questions you may have.

e. Set Ground Rules: Establish clear ground rules and boundaries before engaging in new activities. Discuss what is and isn't off-limits, establish safe words or signals for communicating discomfort or stopping the activity, and agree on a plan for checking in with each other during and after the experience.

f. Focus on Pleasure: Keep the focus on mutual pleasure and enjoyment throughout the process. Encourage each other to communicate openly about what feels good and what doesn't, and be responsive to your partner's needs and feedback.

g. Embrace Experimentation: Be open-minded and willing to explore new ideas and experiences together. Embrace the spirit of experimentation and curiosity, and don't be afraid to step outside of your comfort zones in pursuit of pleasure and connection.

h. Respect Each Other's Limits: Respect each other's limits and boundaries at all times. If either partner expresses discomfort or reluctance during the experience, be prepared to pause or stop altogether and revisit the conversation later.

i. Reflect and Communicate: After trying out new elements, take the time to reflect on the experience together. Share your thoughts, feelings, and feedback with each other in a non-judgmental and constructive manner. Use this opportunity to strengthen your communication and deepen your connection as a couple.

j. Keep It Fun and Lighthearted: Above all, remember to keep the experience fun, playful, and lighthearted. Don't take yourselves too seriously, and approach new experiences with a sense of adventure and curiosity. Enjoy the journey of exploring each other's desires and deepening your bond as a couple.

Chapter Four

The Harsh Realities Relating To Sexual Intimacy

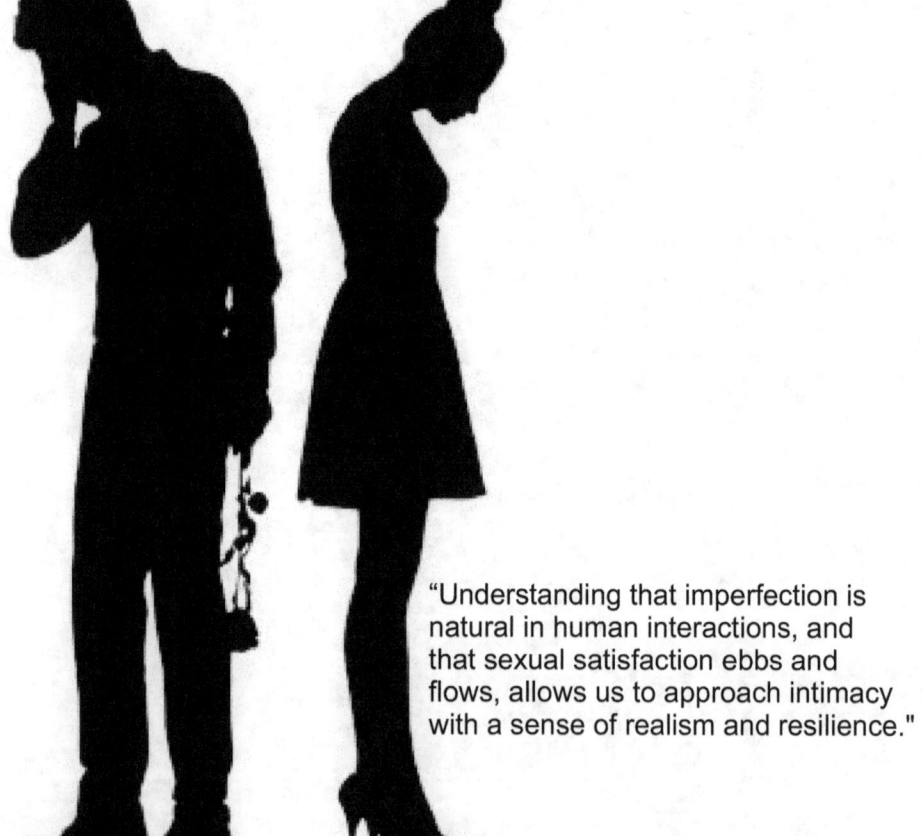

"Understanding that imperfection is natural in human interactions, and that sexual satisfaction ebbs and flows, allows us to approach intimacy with a sense of realism and resilience."

The Harsh Realities Relating To Sexual Intimacy

As we embark on our exploration of the realities of sexual intimacy, it's essential to recognize that understanding these dynamics goes beyond mere curiosity—it can be the key to avoiding major setbacks that may lead to relationship turmoil or even divorce. In a world where the narrative often revolves around perfection and flawlessness in relationships, it's crucial to acknowledge that true compatibility extends beyond the absence of conflict. Instead, it encompasses the recognition that differences are inevitable, and there are certain realities of life that we cannot avoid.

Sexual intimacy, as a cornerstone of romantic partnerships, is not immune to the complexities and challenges that characterize human relationships. By delving into the less glamorous aspects of sexual connection, we equip ourselves with the tools necessary to navigate the inevitable hurdles that may arise. Understanding that imperfection is natural in human interactions, and that sexual satisfaction ebbs and flows, allows us to approach intimacy with a sense of realism and resilience.

Furthermore, recognizing the phases and transitions that mark the journey of a prolonged relationship—from the euphoria of newfound love to the challenges of parenthood and aging—empowers us to anticipate and adapt to changes with grace and understanding. By acknowledging the external pressures and stressors that can impact sexual intimacy, we learn to cultivate empathy and support for our partners, creating a deeper sense of connection and solidarity.

Ultimately, by embracing the realities of sexual intimacy, we open ourselves up to a richer, more nuanced understanding of ourselves and our partners. Through honest communication, mutual respect, and a willingness to confront challenges head-on, we pave the way for greater intimacy, fulfillment, and longevity in our relationships. So, let us journey forth with an open heart and mind, ready to explore the depths of sexual intimacy and emerge stronger and more connected than ever before.

Despite our desires for perfection and fulfillment, the realities of life often present challenges that impact our sexual experiences. Here, we confront these truths head-on, acknowledging that while they may not be ideal, they are a natural part of the human experience

Imperfect Satisfaction

Love isn't just a short-lived feeling; it's also a conscious decision we make every day. In the ebb and flow of emotions, there are moments when feelings can be unpredictable, even moody; here today and nowhere to be found tomorrow. They might hesitate, fluctuate, or even disappear momentarily. But amidst these emotional rushes, it is choice that holds us together and keep us standing in our commitment to love the other person.

The concept of the 80/20 rule illustrates this beautifully. It suggests that while our partners may not embody every quality we desire, they often possess attributes that make them perfectly suited for us. In other words, no one is perfect, and relationships thrive not because of flawless compatibility but because of the willingness to accept and appreciate each other's differences.

Moreover, love as a choice serves as a guiding light in tumultuous times. When emotions run high and doubts creep in, our conscious decision to love reminds us why we chose our partners in the first place. Even when feelings may temporarily fade, our commitment to the relationship keeps us anchored.

For instance, during moments of anger or frustration, our choice to love allows us to see beyond the immediate conflict. We understand that our partners are flawed yet inherently valuable, and their presence enriches our lives in profound ways. This acknowledgment reinforces our commitment to the relationship, even in the face of adversity.

In essence, the 80/20 rule emphasizes the importance of embracing imperfections and choosing to love despite them. It's a reflection of the enduring power of love—a love that goes beyond the short-lived emotions and endures through the highs and lows of life's journey.

It is essential to acknowledge that no partner can fully satisfy our every need or expectation. This reality may initially seem daunting, but it's a fundamental aspect of any relationship. Instead of seeking perfection, we must embrace imperfection and recognize that our partners, like ourselves, are flawed beings.

Despite this inherent imperfection, the key to a successful relationship lies in our ability to choose love over momentary feelings of dissatisfaction. While the 20% of shortcomings may occasionally surface, they should never overshadow the 80% of strengths and qualities that make our partners invaluable to us.

Therefore, let us embrace the reality that our partners will not always meet our every desire, but let us also celebrate the multitude of ways in which they enrich our lives. By focusing on the abundance rather than the scarcity, we can cultivate a deep and enduring love that withstands the test of time.

Inconsistent Awesomeness

Contrary to the often glamorized portrayals in media and popular culture, the reality is that sexual experiences won't always be the stuff of fairy tales. Like any facet of life, there are bound to be fluctuations in the quality and intensity of our intimate encounters. Various factors, ranging from external stressors to internal dynamics within the relationship, can significantly impact the way we experience and perceive sex.

Consider the effects of stress—an ever-present presence in modern life—on our sexual well-being. When struggling with work pressures, financial concerns, or family obligations, our minds may struggle to fully engage in the present moment, hindering our ability to experience pleasure and intimacy to the fullest extent. Similarly, fatigue resulting from hectic schedules or physical exhaustion can dampen our libido and diminish our enthusiasm for sexual activity.

Moreover, the dynamics within the relationship itself play a crucial role in shaping our sexual experiences. Communication breakdowns, unresolved conflicts, or emotional distance between partners can create barriers to intimacy, leading to feelings of dissatisfaction or disconnection in the bedroom.

Yet, it's essential to recognize that these fluctuations are not indicative of failure or inadequacy within the relationship. Instead, they represent the natural complexities of human experience and the dynamic nature of intimate connection. By acknowledging and embracing the ebb and flow of sexual intimacy, couples can cultivate resilience and strengthen their bond beyond mere physical pleasure.

Navigating the highs and lows of sexual experiences together creates a deeper understanding and acceptance of each other's needs and desires. It opens the door to honest communication, vulnerability, and mutual support, laying the foundation for a more fulfilling and enriching relationship.

It's crucial for couples to understand that while sexual intimacy is undoubtedly an important part of any romantic relationship, it should not serve as the only measure of the relationship's success. By placing undue emphasis on sexual performance or satisfaction, couples risk overlooking many other dimensions of their connection, such as emotional intimacy, shared values, and mutual respect.

The Harsh Realities Relating To Sexual Intimacy

Relationships succeed when partners prioritize holistic intimacy, involving not only physical closeness but also emotional connection, intellectual stimulation, and shared experiences. By nurturing these different facets of intimacy, couples can deepen their bond and weather the inevitable challenges that arise in their sexual journey together.

Ultimately, by embracing the multidimensional nature of sexual intimacy and approaching it with compassion, curiosity, and a willingness to adapt, couples can embark on a journey of exploration and growth that exceeds the short-lived appeal for perfection and embrace the beauty of imperfection.

Phases of Prolonged Relationships

Long-term relationships are a journey marked by different phases, each presenting its own set of challenges and opportunities for growth. From the initial spark of infatuation to the realities of navigating life's trials and tribulations together, couples go through different experiences that shape their bond and influence their sexual intimacy.

Honeymoon Phase: As couples pass through the bliss of the honeymoon phase, they may find themselves exploring new facets of their sexuality and indulging in fantasies they may have never dared to share before. The exhilarating sense of liberation and uninhibited desire creates an environment conducive to adventurous experimentation and uninhibited exploration. Partners may delight in discovering each other's preferences, quirks, and hidden desires, creating a sense of intimacy and connection that goes beyond the physical realm.

However, as the initial frenzy of passion begins to varnish, couples may encounter the sobering reality of navigating the complexities of everyday life together. The demands of work, family obligations, and other responsibilities can gradually affect the calm bubble of the honeymoon phase, challenging couples to sustain the intensity of their connection amidst the realities of daily existence. Despite the inevitable ebbs and flows, couples who actively prioritize their relationship and invest in nurturing their emotional bond can weather the transition from infatuation to enduring love, laying the groundwork for a resilient and fulfilling partnership.

Transitioning to Stability: During this phase, couples transition from the euphoric highs of infatuation to a more grounded sense of stability and security. While the fiery passion of the honeymoon phase may calm down, it is replaced by a sense of emotional intimacy and mutual understanding. Partners become attuned to each other's needs, preferences, and characteristics, creating a deeper connection that goes beyond the short-lived excitement of initial attraction.

As the initial passion of romance gives way to a more settled routine, couples may find themselves exploring new dimensions of intimacy beyond the physical realm. Shared experiences, inside jokes, and cherished memories serve as the building blocks of their bond, anchoring them to each other amidst life's inevitable challenges and uncertainties. While the frequency of sexual encounters may fluctuate, the quality of intimacy deepens as partners learn to communicate openly, express vulnerability, and prioritize each other's well-being.

Despite the inevitable shifts and adjustments that accompany the transition to stability, couples who approach this phase with patience, empathy, and a willingness to grow together can cultivate a relationship that withstands the test of time. By embracing the evolving nature of intimacy and remaining committed to nurturing their connection, couples can embark on a journey of enduring love and mutual fulfillment, savoring the beauty of companionship that exceeds the short-lived allure of passion.

Navigating the Journey of Parenthood: Embarking on the journey of parenthood marks a significant milestone in the life of a couple, ushering in a period of transformation and growth. The arrival of children brings immeasurable joy and fulfillment, as couples embrace the role of

The Harsh Realities Relating To Sexual Intimacy

nurturing and guiding new life into the world. However, amidst the countless blessings of parenthood, couples also encounter a lot of challenges that can strain their relationship and impact sexual intimacy.

One of the most common challenges faced by parents is the overwhelming demands of caregiving, particularly during the early years of a child's life. Sleepless nights, round-the-clock feeding sessions, and the relentless cycle of diaper changes can leave parents feeling exhausted and depleted, leaving little time or energy for intimate connection. Moreover, the emotional and physical toll of parenthood can contribute to feelings of stress, anxiety, and self-doubt, further exacerbating the strain on the relationship.

Additionally, the shifting dynamics of family life can create logistical challenges that disrupt the couple's ability to prioritize their relationship. Balancing childcare responsibilities, household chores, and professional obligations often leaves couples feeling stretched thin, with little opportunity for quality time together. As a result, sexual intimacy may take a backseat to more pressing demands, leading to feelings of neglect or dissatisfaction.

Despite these challenges, couples can find solace in the knowledge that they are not alone in their struggles. By creating open communication, mutual support, and a willingness to adapt, couples can navigate the ups and downs of parenthood together, strengthening their bond in the process. Moreover, prioritizing self-care and figure out dedicated time for intimacy can help couples reconnect on a deeper level, reaffirming their commitment to each other amidst the joys and challenges of raising a family.

In essence, while parenthood undoubtedly presents its fair share of obstacles to sexual intimacy, it also offers couples an opportunity to deepen their connection and strengthen their relationship in ways they never thought possible. By embracing the journey of parenthood with patience, resilience, and a sense of shared purpose, couples can weather the storms together and emerge stronger and more united than ever before.

Navigating Financial Hardships: Amidst the journey of building a life together, couples may encounter the daunting reality of financial hardships, which can cast a shadow over their intimate connection. Economic downturns, job loss, or unforeseen expenses can unleash a wave of stress and uncertainty, placing immense strain on the relationship and dampening the flames of love.

The relentless pressure to make ends meet and the constant worry about the future can blur moments of intimacy and passion, as couples find themselves consumed by the demands of financial survival. The weight of financial burdens can permeate every aspect of life, leaving little room for the spontaneity and joy that once characterized their relationship.

Yet, amidst the chaos of financial turmoil, couples have the opportunity to forge a deeper bond rooted in resilience and mutual support. By confronting these challenges head-on and facing them together as a united front, couples can discover a newfound strength in their partnership. Sharing the burden of financial hardship can create a sense of solidarity and camaraderie, as couples lean on each other for emotional support and practical solutions.

Moreover, navigating financial challenges can serve as a catalyst for growth and transformation within the relationship. It offers couples the chance to reassess their priorities, redefine their goals, and cultivate a greater sense of gratitude for the blessings they share. Through open communication, honest dialogue, and a willingness to adapt, couples can find creative ways to weather the storm and emerge stronger and more resilient than ever before.

Ultimately, while financial hardships may pose significant obstacles to sexual intimacy, they also present an opportunity for couples to deepen their connection and reaffirm their commitment to each other. By embracing the journey of financial recovery with patience, perseverance, and unwavering support, couples can navigate these turbulent waters together and emerge stronger, more united, and more deeply in love than ever before.

Embracing Change and Growth: As couples journey through the various phases of a prolonged relationship, they are called upon to embrace change and growth, both individually and as a partnership. Recognizing and acknowledging the natural evolution of their bond is essential for navigating the complexities of sexual intimacy with grace and resilience.

One of the keys to navigating change within a relationship is prioritizing communication. Couples must be willing to openly discuss their evolving needs, desires, and concerns, creating a sense of understanding and empathy between them. By maintaining open lines of communication, couples can address challenges as they arise and work together to find mutually satisfying solutions.

Empathy plays a crucial role in navigating the changes that come with a prolonged relationship. Partners must strive to understand each other's perspectives and experiences, even when they differ from their own. By practicing empathy, couples can cultivate a deeper sense of connection and intimacy, establishing a bond that withstands the test of time.

Mutual respect is another cornerstone of a thriving relationship, particularly when it comes to sexual intimacy. Couples must honor each other's boundaries, preferences, and autonomy, ensuring that their interactions are built on a foundation of trust and mutual consent. By prioritizing respect, couples can create a safe and supportive environment for exploring their sexual connection.

Ultimately, by embracing change and growth within their relationship, couples can forge a lasting connection that transcends the passage of time. Through communication, empathy, and mutual respect, couples can navigate the complexities of sexual intimacy with grace and resilience, building a foundation for a fulfilling and enriching partnership.

Coping with Aging: As couples journey through life together, they inevitably encounter the profound transformations that come with aging. The passage of time brings with it many changes, both physical and emotional, that can profoundly impact sexual intimacy and redefine the dynamics of the relationship.

One of the most significant challenges that couples face as they age is the gradual decline in physical health and vitality. As bodies mature and undergo natural wear and tear, individuals may find themselves struggling with a range of age-related health issues, from arthritis and joint pain to chronic conditions such as diabetes or heart disease. These physical ailments can not only affect one's overall well-being but also take a toll on sexual function and desire, making it more difficult to engage in intimate activities with the same vigor and frequency as in years past.

In addition to physical health concerns, aging also brings about hormonal changes that can further complicate matters when it comes to sexual intimacy. Fluctuations in hormone levels, particularly in menopause or andropause, can lead to symptoms such as decreased libido, vaginal dryness, erectile dysfunction, and mood swings, all of which can impact one's ability to engage in sexual activity and experience pleasure.

Furthermore, as couples navigate the ups and downs of aging together, they may find themselves contending with shifts in their sexual desires and preferences. What once brought excitement and pleasure may no longer hold the same appeal, leading couples to explore new avenues of intimacy and connection. Communication becomes key during this phase of life, as partners must openly discuss their changing needs and desires, and work together to find mutually satisfying ways to maintain intimacy and connection.

Despite the challenges that come with aging, many couples discover that their bond deepens with time, as they cherish the shared memories and experiences that have shaped their journey together. They may find solace in the comfort and familiarity of each other's presence, and derive pleasure from the simple acts of affection and companionship that define their relationship. In embracing the realities of aging with grace and resilience, couples can cultivate a love that transcends the physical and endures through the passage of time.

External Pressures and Stressors

Beyond the confines of the relationship, couples often find themselves contending with many external pressures and stressors that can exert a significant influence on sexual intimacy. From the demands of work and career aspirations to the responsibilities of raising a family and managing household affairs, navigating these external pressures requires couples to strike a delicate balance between various competing priorities.

Work stress, in particular, can be a pervasive factor that impacts sexual intimacy. The pressures of deadlines, long hours, and career aspirations can leave individuals feeling mentally and physically exhausted, making it challenging to muster the energy and enthusiasm for sex with their partner. Moreover, the blurring of boundaries between work and personal life in today's hyperconnected world can further increase stress levels, leaving little room for relaxation and sex.

Family obligations also play a significant role in shaping the landscape of sexual intimacy within a relationship. Whether it's caring for aging parents, attending to the needs of children, or managing extended family dynamics, couples may find themselves stretched thin as they strive to fulfill their familial duties. The demands of caregiving and household responsibilities can leave couples feeling drained and overwhelmed, leaving little time or energy for nurturing their romantic connection.

Societal expectations and norms surrounding sex and intimacy can also exert subtle yet powerful influence on couples' sexual experiences. From cultural taboos and gender stereotypes to unrealistic portrayals of romance and sexuality in the media, couples may find themselves struggling with external pressures that shape their perceptions and expectations of sex. Overcoming these societal pressures requires couples to challenge conventional norms and create a more open and inclusive dialogue about sex and intimacy within their relationship.

Navigating these external pressures and stressors requires couples to cultivate patience, empathy, and effective communication. By acknowledging the impact of external factors on their sexual intimacy, couples can work together to establish boundaries, prioritize self-care, and create quality time for nurturing their connection. By supporting each other through life's challenges and uncertainties, couples can strengthen their bond and create a resilient foundation for intimacy and mutual fulfillment.

Navigating Differences

In the realm of sexual intimacy, each individual comes with their own unique set of desires, fantasies, and boundaries. These differences can manifest in various ways, ranging from preferred sexual activities and frequency of intimacy to communication styles and comfort levels with experimentation. Navigating these differences requires couples to approach their sexual relationship with mutual respect, empathy, and a genuine willingness to understand and accommodate each other's needs and preferences.

Mutual respect forms the cornerstone of navigating differences in sexual intimacy. It involves recognizing and valuing each other's autonomy, agency, and right to express their desires and boundaries without judgment. By fostering an environment of trust and respect, couples can create a safe space where they feel comfortable discussing their sexual preferences and exploring new avenues of intimacy together.

The Harsh Realities Relating To Sexual Intimacy

Compromise is another essential component of navigating differences in sexual intimacy. It entails finding common ground and mutually agreeable solutions that honor both partners' needs and desires. This may involve negotiating compromises, exploring new sexual activities or fantasies that satisfy both partners, or establishing boundaries that respect each other's comfort levels and boundaries.

A willingness to explore and understand each other's perspectives is crucial for navigating differences in sexual intimacy. This involves engaging in open and honest communication about desires, fantasies, and boundaries, as well as actively listening to and validating each other's experiences and emotions. By cultivating empathy and compassion, couples can bridge the gap between their differences and create a deeper sense of connection and intimacy.

Embracing diversity and celebrating the uniqueness of each partner is key to enriching the sexual experience and strengthening the relationship. Rather than viewing differences as obstacles or sources of conflict, couples can embrace them as opportunities for growth, exploration, and mutual learning. By embracing diversity in sexual preferences, communication styles, and expressions of intimacy, couples can create a rich and fulfilling sexual relationship that honors their individuality while deepening their connection as a couple.

As we conclude our exploration of the complexities of sexual intimacy within prolonged relationships, it's imperative to underscore the importance of understanding and accepting the realities we cannot change. In a world where societal narratives often portray relationships through a lens of perfection, it's crucial to recognize that true compatibility goes beyond the absence of conflict and involves the acknowledgment of differences and inevitable challenges.

Our journey has revealed that sexual intimacy is a multifaceted aspect of romantic partnerships, influenced by various internal and external factors. From the initial euphoria of infatuation to the challenges of parenthood, financial hardships, and the inevitable changes that come with aging, couples encounter a diverse array of experiences that shape their bond and influence their sexual connection.

Let me share with you the story of Dally and Simon. After Dally fell pregnant, the couple began experiencing challenges, particularly as Simon struggled to cope with the emotional changes accompanying her pregnancy. This highlights the importance of understanding and preparing for the significant life transitions that can impact sexual intimacy within a relationship. I have always maintained that couples must normalize going for Pre-Pregnancy counseling, as most men are unprepared to handle the hormonal changes that come with their partner's pregnancy. Lack of understanding and preparation for these emotional changes can lead to relationship strain and potential collapse.

Amidst these challenges, however, stable relationships offer a source of solace and support. By prioritizing effective communication, empathy, and mutual respect, couples can navigate the complexities of sexual intimacy with grace and resilience. Moreover, maintaining stable relationships can significantly benefit our overall well-being, providing a sense of security, belonging, and fulfillment that surpasses the short-lived nature of sexual satisfaction.

In essence, our journey has underscored the importance of embracing the realities of sexual intimacy within prolonged relationships. By approaching intimacy with a sense of realism, patience, and understanding, couples can cultivate a love that transcends the physical and endures through the passage of time. So let us embark on our journey with open hearts and minds, ready to confront the challenges and celebrate the joys of sexual intimacy within the context of enduring love and partnership.

Chapter Five

Redefining Sexual Intimacy

"Sexual intimacy is an emotional dance of erotic energies that connects two souls and ignites a profound connection between them."

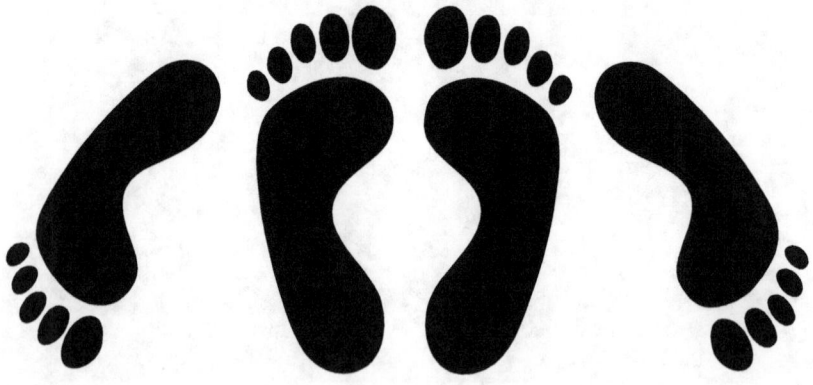

Redefining Sexual Intimacy

Sexual intimacy has traditionally been narrowly defined within the confines of genital penetration, often overlooking the rich experiences that contribute to fulfilling and meaningful connections between partners. While the physical act of intercourse undoubtedly holds significance within the realm of sexual expression, it represents just one facet of a much broader spectrum of intimate encounters.

In this chapter, we embark on a journey to redefine sexual intimacy, challenging conventional notions and exploring the innumerable ways in which partners can connect intimately beyond traditional penetrative sex. By expanding our understanding of what constitutes sexual intimacy, we open ourselves up to a world of possibilities, where pleasure, connection, and fulfillment can be found in diverse forms of erotic exploration.

Central to this exploration is the recognition that sexuality is inherently multifaceted, encompassing a wide range of sensations, emotions, and interactions. By breaking free from restrictive definitions and embracing the complexity of human desire, we empower ourselves to explore and celebrate the full spectrum of our sexual experiences.

Sexual intimacy is an emotional dance of erotic energies that connects two souls and ignite a profound connection between them. Beyond mere physical pleasure, sexual intimacy is a deeply human experience that encompasses the merging of hearts, minds, and spirits, echoing what is biblically defined as, "The two shall become one flesh."

At its core, sexual intimacy is a powerful energy that binds individuals together in a unique and transformative way. It is a fusion of desires, emotions, and sensations that goes beyond the boundaries of the physical body, enveloping partners in a cocoon of shared vulnerability and ecstasy.

To confine sexual intimacy solely to the realm of intercourse is to overlook its true essence and the countless ways in which it can enrich our lives. Indeed, the pleasure derived from sexual intimacy extends far beyond the short lived ecstasy of orgasm. It lies in the intimate connection forged between partners, the shared moments of tenderness and passion, and the profound sense of unity that arises from the merging of souls.

In essence, sexual intimacy is a gateway to a world of boundless togetherness—a realm where partners can explore, discover, and celebrate the depths of their connection without embarrassment or restraint. It is a sacred space where the barriers between self and other dissolve, giving rise to a profound sense of intimacy, belonging, and fulfillment.

By expanding our understanding of sexual intimacy beyond the confines of intercourse, we open ourselves up to a wealth of possibilities for connection, exploration, and growth. It is through embracing the full spectrum of erotic energies that we unlock the true potential of sexual intimacy and embark on a journey of profound discovery and mutual fulfillment.

Orgasms Killed Sex!

In recent times, there has been a pervasive cultural narrative that places undue emphasis on the pursuit of orgasm as the ultimate goal of sexual intimacy. This narrow focus on climaxing has led many individuals to approach sex with a sense of urgency and performance anxiety, robbing them of the opportunity to fully immerse themselves in the experience of intimacy.

The relentless pressure to achieve orgasm, coupled with the expectation of simultaneous pleasure for both partners, has created an environment where the true meaning of sexual intimacy is often lost. Instead of savoring the journey of exploration and connection, individuals find themselves fixated on the end goal, racing towards climax without truly experiencing the depths of intimacy along the way.

This fixation on achieving orgasm as the ultimate goal of sexual intimacy creates a relentless cycle of pressure and anxiety that can significantly reduce the overall pleasure and satisfaction of the experience. When individuals approach sex with the sole focus of reaching orgasm, they often set unrealistic expectations for themselves and their partners. This intense pressure to perform and meet these expectations can lead to heightened anxiety and stress, which are significant barriers to sexual arousal and enjoyment.

As the pursuit of orgasm becomes the primary objective, individuals may find themselves hyper-focused on reaching this goal, losing sight of the present moment and the intimate connection with their partner. This tunnel vision can prevent them from fully experiencing the sensations and emotions of the sexual encounter, leading to a sense of disconnection and dissatisfaction.

Moreover, the pressure to orgasm can create a sense of inadequacy and self-doubt when expectations are not met. Individuals may internalize feelings of failure or incompetence, believing that their inability to reach orgasm reflects negatively on their worth as a sexual partner. This negative self-perception can erode confidence and self-esteem, further increasing feelings of frustration and disappointment.

In addition, the anxiety and pressure associated with the pursuit of pleasure can hinder sexual arousal and responsiveness, making it more difficult for both men and women to reach orgasm. Performance anxiety can interfere with the body's natural sexual response cycle, leading to difficulties in achieving and maintaining arousal, as well as delays in orgasm or an inability to climax altogether.

This cycle of disappointment and disillusionment can perpetuate negative patterns of behavior and communication within a relationship.

Partners may feel disconnected from each other, unable to effectively communicate their needs and desires due to feelings of shame or embarrassment. This breakdown in communication can further increase feelings of inadequacy and frustration, creating a cycle of sexual dissatisfaction within the relationship.

Ultimately, the relentless pursuit of orgasm at the expense of genuine intimacy and connection can have detrimental effects on both individuals and their relationships. Breaking free from this cycle requires a shift in mindset towards embracing the full spectrum of sexual experiences and prioritizing pleasure, connection, and mutual satisfaction over performance-driven goals.

Furthermore, the cultural emphasis on penetrative sex as the primary means of achieving orgasm overlooks the diverse ways in which individuals experience pleasure. Research has shown that the majority of women do not orgasm through penetrative sex alone, highlighting the limitations of this narrow definition of sexual satisfaction.

In a society where sexual compatibility is often measured by one's ability to achieve orgasm through penetration, couples may feel immense pressure to conform to unrealistic expectations, leading to feelings of inadequacy and self-doubt. This emphasis on performance-based satisfaction can erode the foundation of trust and intimacy within a relationship, causing individuals to question their worth and desirability.

Ultimately, the relentless pursuit of orgasm at the expense of true intimacy has led many to miss out on the deeper pleasures of sexual connection. By shifting the focus away from performance and towards presence, couples can cultivate a more meaningful and fulfilling experience of intimacy that goes beyond the limitations of orgasm-centric sex.

Sex Is A Journey

Sexual intimacy is best likened to a voyage—a journey of discovery and exploration where the destination is not a predetermined endpoint, but rather a series of experiences and connections along the way. Like a treasure hunt in the depths of a forest, sex invites us to embark on an adventure filled with mystery, excitement, and endless possibilities.

In this forest of intimacy, every touch, every caress, and every whispered word is a clue leading us closer to the hidden treasures of pleasure and connection. Each moment of vulnerability and shared vulnerability is a precious gem waiting to be unearthed, enriching our experience and deepening our bond with our partner.

By embracing sex as a journey rather than a race, we free ourselves from the constraints of performance and expectation, allowing us to fully immerse ourselves in the richness of the journey. Instead of focusing on the end goal of orgasm, we savor each moment along the way, relishing in the sensations, emotions, and connections that unfold in the present.

Just as a treasure hunt requires patience, perseverance, and an open mind, so too does sexual intimacy. It is a journey filled with twists and turns, highs and lows, but also moments of profound connection and ecstasy. By embracing the unknown and surrendering to the experience, couples can unlock the true potential of their intimacy and forge a deeper bond with each other.

In this spirit of exploration, we discover that true fulfillment lies not in reaching a predetermined destination, but in the journey itself—the shared experiences, the deepening connection, and the profound sense of intimacy that emerges when we surrender to the flow of the moment.

So let us set sail on this voyage of sexual intimacy with open hearts and curious minds, ready to explore the depths of desire and connection that await us. Together, let us uncover the hidden treasures of pleasure, passion, and love that lie waiting to be discovered in the forest of intimacy.

Sexual Intimacy Is A Soul Affair!

Sexual intimacy is a profound interplay of the mind, the heart, and the body—a deeply soulful affair that transcends mere physicality. As we delve into the essence of sexual connection, we must recognize that it encompasses a multitude of dimensions, each connected to the fabric of our human experience.

Traditionally, sexual intimacy has been narrowly defined within the boundaries of genital penetration, overlooking the vast array of experiences that contribute to deep and meaningful connections between partners. While intercourse holds significance, it represents just one facet of a much broader spectrum of intimate encounters.

As we embark on a journey to redefine sexual intimacy, we challenge conventional notions and we explore a thousand ways in which partners can connect intimately beyond traditional penetrative sex. By expanding our understanding of what constitutes sexual intimacy, we open ourselves up to a world of possibilities, where pleasure, connection, and fulfillment can be found in diverse forms of erotic exploration.

Central to this exploration is the acknowledgment of the complex interplay between the mind, the heart, and the body in sexual expression. I want us to look into these dimensions and how they play a role in our intimate moments.

The Mind

The mind, often referred to as the seat of desire and imagination, plays a crucial role in shaping our sexual experiences. It is where fantasies are born, and desires are kindled. Through the power of imagination, partners can create rich and elaborate scenarios that heighten arousal and deepen connection.

Redefining Sexual Intimacy

In sexual intimacy, the mind acts as a canvas upon which desires are painted and passions are ignited. Anticipation builds as partners engage in playful banter or exchange flirtatious glances, each interaction fueling the flames of desire. In this state of heightened arousal, inhibitions dissolve, paving the way for uninhibited exploration and connection.

Partners can engage in the art of mental foreplay, tantalizing each other's senses with vivid imagery and tantalizing descriptions. Whether through whispered fantasies, steamy text messages, or erotic storytelling, the mind becomes a playground for sensual exploration, where boundaries are pushed and inhibitions are left behind.

Moreover, the mind allows partners to engage in acts of virtual intimacy, where physical proximity is not a barrier to connection. Through the power of technology, couples can engage in activities such as telephone sex or video calls, where the mind becomes the primary tool for stimulation.

Telephone sex, in particular, relies heavily on the imagination and the power of suggestion. Partners can describe their desires and fantasies in vivid detail, painting a picture with words that evokes intense arousal and excitement. Despite being physically apart, the mental connection forged through telephone sex can be just as potent and fulfilling as physical intimacy.

From whispered confessions to shared fantasies, the mind serves as a channel for erotic expression, allowing partners to romance and seduce each other with nothing more than their thoughts and words. In this soulish dance of sexual intimacy, the mind becomes a powerful instrument of connection, binding partners together in a shared experience of desire, passion, and pleasure.

When the mind is not actively involved in sexual intimacy, the experience may become mechanical or routine, devoid of passion and spontaneity. Partners may go through the motions without fully connecting with each other on an emotional or intellectual level, leading to a sense of disconnection and dissatisfaction.

Without the engagement of the mind, sexual encounters may lack creativity and imagination, resulting in a repetitive and uninspired routine. Fantasies remain unexplored, desires go unfulfilled, and the full potential of intimacy remains untapped.

Furthermore, the absence of mental engagement can contribute to feelings of boredom or monotony in the bedroom. Partners may struggle to maintain interest and excitement in their sexual interactions, leading to a decline in desire and arousal over time.

In some cases, the neglect of the mind in sexual intimacy can lead to performance anxiety or insecurities. Without the ability to engage in meaningful communication or express desires openly, partners may feel pressure to meet unrealistic expectations or perform to a certain standard, leading to feelings of inadequacy and self-doubt.

Moreover, when the mind is not utilized in sexual intimacy, partners may miss out on the opportunity to deepen their emotional connection and intimacy. Communication becomes limited, inhibiting the sharing of desires, fantasies, and vulnerabilities that are essential for building trust and intimacy.

In conclusion, the absence of mental engagement in sexual intimacy can significantly hinder the depth, connection, and fulfillment that partners seek in their relationships. However, by actively involving the mind in sexual encounters, couples have the opportunity to enhance their experience, deepen their connection, and explore new dimensions of pleasure and intimacy together.

Embracing the role of the mind in sexual intimacy opens the door to a richer, more meaningful experience, where desires are shared, fantasies are explored, and emotional connections are strengthened. Ultimately, by recognizing the importance of mental engagement, couples can cultivate a more fulfilling and satisfying sexual relationship that nourishes both their physical desires and emotional bond.

The Heart

The heart, meanwhile, serves as the locus of emotion and vulnerability—the wellspring of love, trust, and intimacy. It is through the heart that we open ourselves to another, laying bare our deepest desires, fears, and vulnerabilities.

In the realm of sexual intimacy, the heart plays a crucial role, serving as a compass that guides us towards moments of tenderness, passion, and profound connection. When the heart is fully engaged, it infuses every touch, every caress, and every whispered word with meaning and depth.

It allows us to connect with our partner on a deeply emotional level, fostering a sense of closeness and intimacy that transcends the physical act itself. Moreover, the heart's involvement in sexual intimacy creates a safe space for vulnerability and authenticity, allowing partners to express themselves fully and without reservation.

In essence, the heart is the seat of emotional connection in sexual intimacy, anchoring the experience in love, trust, and mutual respect. As such, nurturing the heart's involvement in sexual encounters is essential for nurturing deep, meaningful connections and fulfilling relationships.

By prioritizing emotional connection and vulnerability, couples can create an environment where intimacy flourishes, deepening their bond and enhancing their sexual experiences. When the heart is fully engaged, partners can explore new dimensions of pleasure and connection, enriching their relationship and creating lasting memories of intimacy and love.

On the other hand, when the heart is absent or underutilized in sexual intimacy, the experience can lack depth, connection, and emotional fulfillment. Without the heart's involvement, sexual encounters may become purely physical, devoid of emotional resonance and meaning.

Partners may find themselves going through the act without truly connecting on an emotional level, leading to feelings of emptiness, disconnection, and dissatisfaction. In the absence of emotional engagement, sexual encounters may feel shallow and transactional, leaving both partners craving a deeper connection.

Moreover, the absence of the heart in sexual intimacy can contribute to a sense of detachment and emotional distance between partners. Without emotional vulnerability and authenticity, couples may struggle to communicate their needs and desires effectively, leading to misunderstandings, resentment, and conflict.

Additionally, when the heart is not fully engaged, partners may be more susceptible to feelings of insecurity, mistrust, and loneliness within the relationship. Without the emotional connection that comes from engaging the heart in sexual intimacy, couples may feel disconnected from each other, leading to a breakdown in intimacy and closeness over time.

Ultimately, the absence of the heart in sexual intimacy can have profound implications for the health and longevity of a relationship. Without emotional connection and vulnerability, couples may struggle to maintain intimacy and fulfillment, leading to dissatisfaction and potentially the erosion of the relationship itself.

Therefore, prioritizing the involvement of the heart in sexual encounters is essential for creating deep, meaningful connections and fulfilling relationships. By nurturing emotional connection and vulnerability, couples can create an environment where intimacy flourishes, enhancing their sexual experiences and strengthening their bond with each other.

In essence, the heart plays a vital role in sexual intimacy, serving as the compass that guides us towards deeper connection, vulnerability, and emotional fulfillment. When the heart is fully engaged, sexual encounters transcend mere physicality, becoming profound expressions of love, trust, and intimacy.

By opening ourselves to the vulnerability of the heart, we invite a deeper level of connection and intimacy into our sexual experiences. When partners approach intimacy with authenticity, empathy, and emotional presence, they create a sacred space where true connection can flourish.

In embracing the presence of the heart in sexual intimacy, couples unlock the potential for profound emotional and spiritual connection, enriching their relationship and deepening their bond with each other. Through the fusion of heart, mind, and body, partners embark on a journey of mutual exploration, passion, and fulfillment, celebrating the beauty and complexity of their shared intimacy.

Ultimately, by honoring the presence of the heart in sexual encounters, couples cultivate a deeper understanding of themselves and each other, building intimacy, trust, and love that goes beyond the physical realm. It is through the integration of heart-centered intimacy that partners discover the true essence of sexual connection—a journey of profound discovery, vulnerability, and boundless love.

The body

The body is the vessel through which we experience the physical sensations of sexual intimacy. It serves as the channel for pleasure, arousal, and sensory exploration, allowing us to fully engage in the physical aspects of sexual connection.

In the realm of sexual intimacy, the body becomes a canvas upon which desire is expressed and pleasure is received. Through touch, caress, and physical contact, partners communicate their attraction, affection, and desire for one another.

The senses play a crucial role in the body's involvement in sexual intimacy, as they heighten our awareness and sensitivity to the pleasures of touch, taste, smell, sight, and sound. Each sensory experience contributes to the overall sexual pleasure, enhancing the depth and richness of the intimate encounter.

Moreover, the body's response to sexual stimulation is a complex interplay of physiological and psychological factors. Arousal triggers a cascade of physical responses, including increased heart rate, blood flow to erogenous zones, and the release of neurotransmitters such as dopamine and oxytocin, which enhance pleasure and deepen emotional connection.

The body's involvement in sexual intimacy is not limited to physical arousal; it also encompasses the expression of emotions, desires, and vulnerabilities through non-verbal communication. Body language, gestures, and facial expressions convey messages of desire, passion, and intimacy, enriching the emotional dimension of the sexual encounter.

Erotic zones, also known as erogenous zones or pleasure spots, are areas of the body that are particularly sensitive to sexual stimulation and can elicit pleasurable sensations when touched, kissed, or caressed. These zones play a crucial role in sexual intimacy as they contribute to arousal, pleasure, and the overall experience of physical connection between partners.

While the most commonly recognized erogenous zones include areas such as the genitals, breasts, and lips, the body is actually dotted with a multitude of these zones, each with its own unique sensitivity and potential for pleasure. From the scalp to the toes, every part of the body has the potential to elicit pleasurable sensations when touched with care and intention.

For example, the scalp is a surprisingly sensitive erogenous zone for many individuals. Gentle stroking or massaging of the scalp can stimulate nerve endings and release tension, contributing to relaxation and arousal. Similarly, the back of the neck and the ears are often overlooked erogenous zones that can be highly sensitive to touch and kissing.

Moving down the body, the inner thighs and lower abdomen are also erogenous zones that can be highly sensitive to stimulation. Light caresses and kisses in these areas can heighten arousal and anticipation, setting the stage for further exploration.

Even the feet and toes, often overlooked in discussions of erogenous zones, can be surprisingly sensitive to touch and stimulation. Massaging, kissing, and gentle caresses of the feet and toes can elicit pleasurable sensations and contribute to overall arousal.

Exploring and stimulating these erogenous zones can add variety and excitement to sexual encounters, enhancing pleasure and deepening intimacy between partners. However, it's important to remember that individual preferences and sensitivities vary, so communication and consent are key when exploring erogenous zones with a partner. By paying attention to each other's cues and feedback, couples can discover new ways of experiencing pleasure and connection together.

However, the body's involvement in sexual intimacy is not without its challenges. Issues such as body image insecurities, physical discomfort, and health concerns can impact one's ability to fully engage in sexual encounters. These challenges highlight the importance of creating a safe and supportive environment where partners can communicate openly and address any concerns or insecurities that may arise.

So, the body plays a central role in sexual intimacy, serving as the vehicle through which we experience pleasure, connection, and physical expression. By honoring the body's needs, desires, and sensitivities, couples can cultivate a deeper understanding of themselves and each other, building intimacy, trust, and fulfillment in their sexual relationships.

In conclusion, the beautiful dance of sexual intimacy relies on the seamless coordination of the mind, heart, and body. When any of these elements are absent or out of sync, the flow of the dance is disrupted, leading to feelings of disconnect and dissatisfaction. Whether it's the mind preoccupied with stress, the heart closed off or guarded, or the body tense and inhibited, each imbalance creates barriers to intimacy and inhibits the depth of connection between partners.

However, when all dimensions—the mind, heart, and body—are aligned and fully engaged, the experience of sexual intimacy becomes a profound expression of love, connection, and mutual pleasure. In this state of alignment, partners are able to move beyond the physical act, delving into new depths of intimacy and fulfillment. It is through this harmonious integration of the mind, heart, and body that couples forge a bond that extends far beyond the confines of the bedroom, enriching every aspect of their relationship and journey together.

The Invitation

In embracing the full spectrum of erotic energies, we invite you to embark on a journey of profound self-discovery and mutual exploration. Challenge the constraints of conventional notions of sexual intimacy and venture into uncharted territories of connection and pleasure. By embracing the multidimensionality of sexual expression and integrating the realms of the mind, heart, and body, you unlock the true potential of intimacy.

Through the fusion of these elements, you pave the way for a transformative experience that transcends the physical act itself. It's about more than just the short-lived moments of pleasure; it's about forging a deep and meaningful bond with your partner—a connection that resonates on a soulful level and enriches every facet of your relationship.

So, let us together embark on this journey of intimacy, where curiosity becomes our compass and vulnerability our guide. Let us peel back the layers of societal conditioning and embrace the raw authenticity of our desires. In doing so, we not only redefine what it means to connect intimately but also empower ourselves to create a relationship that is built on a foundation of trust, understanding, and boundless love.

Chapter Six
The Essence Of Sexual Intimacy

"When the journey, language, lifestyle, and connection of two souls converge, they intertwine in the ultimate dance of sexual intimacy—a symphony of passion, vulnerability, and deep connection."

The Essence Of Sexual Intimacy

In this chapter, we embark on a journey to unveil the essence of sex in its holistic nature—a vibrant energy that pulses through the core of human existence. Sex is not merely a physical act but a potent force capable of enveloping us in its embrace, transforming our lives in profound ways. When harnessed and handled with care, it has the power to elevate us to higher frequencies of consciousness, connecting us to the essence of our being.

An intelligent reader would have already noticed the use of the terminology "sexual intimacy" instead of merely referring to it as "sex" to emphasize the deeper, more profound aspects of the human sexual experience. While the term "sex" often evokes thoughts of physical acts and pleasure, "sexual intimacy" encompasses a broader spectrum of emotions, connections, and experiences.

By framing our exploration within the context of sexual intimacy, we acknowledge that sex is not just about the physical act itself but also about the emotional, psychological, and spiritual dimensions that accompany it. Sexual intimacy encompasses the full range of human experiences related to sexuality, including desire, arousal, vulnerability, trust, and connection.

Sexual energy is a primal force that courses through our veins, driving the perpetuation of our species and shaping the very fabric of human existence. It is a force so strong that it defines our survival, our relationships, and our connection to the world around us. The acceptance and understanding of sexual intimacy as an integral part of human existence are essential for the continuation and evolution of our species.

However, despite its inherent power and significance, sex has often been shrouded in shame, guilt, and taboo, relegated to the realms of secrecy and darkness. Society's attitudes towards sex have been colored by fear, ignorance, and misconceptions, leading many to view it as a dirty or sinful act. This stigma surrounding sex has perpetuated feelings of shame and inadequacy, causing individuals to suppress their desires and deny their true nature.

But sex is not a dirty or demonic sport that should inspire shame or guilt. On the contrary, it is a natural and beautiful expression of our humanity—a sacred dance of intimacy and connection that should be celebrated and honored. By reclaiming sex from the shadows of stigma and embracing it as a vital aspect of our existence, we empower ourselves to live authentically and fully embrace our sexuality.

In this chapter, we challenge the notion that sex is something to be ashamed of, and instead, we invite you to explore the profound beauty and significance of sexual intimacy. We delve into the depths of what sex truly is—a powerful force that has the potential to awaken our senses, expand our consciousness, and deepen our connection to ourselves and others.

By shedding light on the true essence of sex, we aim to dismantle the barriers of shame and guilt that have long surrounded it, and to instead invite you to embrace it as a sacred and transformative aspect of human experience. So let us embark on this journey together, as we uncover the mysteries of sex and reclaim its rightful place as a source of joy, connection, and empowerment in our lives.

Sex is a Journey

Sexual intimacy, a journey from desire to connection, it captures the holistic experience that couples embark on from the initial spark of attraction to the profound connection forged through physical intimacy. This journey begins long before any physical contact occurs, rooted in the way partners communicate, respect, and understand each other.

The Essence Of Sexual Intimacy

Communication serves as the cornerstone of sexual intimacy, laying the foundation for understanding, trust, and mutual desire. It involves open and honest dialogue about desires, boundaries, and fantasies, allowing partners to connect on a deeper level emotionally and intellectually. Through communication, couples express their needs, desires, and vulnerabilities, they create a sense of intimacy and connection that fuels their journey towards sexual fulfillment.

Respect is another essential element of sexual intimacy, encompassing the recognition and honoring of each other's autonomy, boundaries, and desires. It involves treating each other with kindness, empathy, and consideration, creating a safe and supportive environment where both partners feel valued and empowered. Respect paves the way for mutual trust and vulnerability, essential ingredients for meaningful and satisfying sexual experiences.

Understanding plays a crucial role in sexual intimacy, as partners seek to empathize with and appreciate each other's needs, desires, and preferences. It involves active listening, empathy, and attunement to each other's emotional and physical cues, allowing couples to connect on a deeper level and respond to each other's needs with sensitivity and care. Understanding nurtures intimacy and connection, creating a sense of closeness and unity that enhances the sexual experience.

Romance serves as a catalyst for desire, igniting passion and arousal long before any physical intimacy occurs. It encompasses gestures, acts of affection, and expressions of love that create anticipation and excitement, fueling the desire to connect intimately with one's partner. From thoughtful gestures to spontaneous acts of romance, couples cultivate an atmosphere of desire and anticipation that enhances their journey towards sexual fulfillment.

Physical intimacy, culminating in intercourse, represents the pinnacle of the sexual journey, where desire, connection, and passion converge in a moment of profound union. It is the culmination of the emotional, psychological, and physical connection forged through communication, respect, understanding, and romance. Physical intimacy transcends the physical act itself, becoming a sacred expression of love, trust, and vulnerability shared between partners.

The journey to sexual desire is a gradual and intricate process that begins with an initial spark of attraction and evolves into a deep and intimate connection between partners. It starts with a moment of attraction—a glance, a smile, or a shared interest—that ignites the spark of desire. This attraction leads to communication and connection as partners engage in meaningful conversations, sharing their thoughts, feelings, and experiences. Through open and honest communication, they build an emotional bond founded on trust, respect, and vulnerability.

Romance plays a pivotal role in heightening desire and anticipation. Thoughtful gestures, romantic dates, and acts of affection fuel the fire of attraction, creating a sense of excitement and longing for physical intimacy. As desire intensifies, partners engage in sensual exploration and foreplay, gradually building sexual tension and arousal through kissing, touching, and verbal expressions of desire.

With each step, sexual tension continues to mount, reaching its peak as partners experience heightened sensations and a strong longing for physical connection. The journey culminates in intercourse—the ultimate expression of desire, connection, and ecstasy. In this moment of profound union, partners merge both physically and emotionally, solidifying their bond and experiencing the full depth of their intimacy.

Throughout this journey, the gradual buildup of sexual tension demonstrates the power of desire and connection between partners. It is a journey marked by anticipation, exploration, and mutual discovery—a journey that strengthens the bond between partners and deepens their intimacy with each other.

The Essence Of Sexual Intimacy

Sexual intimacy is far more than a mere physical connection or a race to an orgasmic experience. It transcends the confines of the bedroom, encompassing a holistic journey traveled by two souls on a path to ultimate pleasure and fulfillment. This journey is one of profound exploration, connection, and mutual discovery—a sacred voyage that leads to the culmination of the "Big O."

At its core, sexual intimacy is about the merging of hearts, minds, and bodies in a shared experience of love, passion, and ecstasy. It is a journey of deep emotional connection, where partners open themselves to vulnerability and authenticity, allowing them to truly see and be seen by each other. This emotional intimacy forms the foundation upon which the physical expression of desire and pleasure unfolds.

The journey to the "Big O" is not merely about reaching a predetermined endpoint, but rather about savoring each moment of connection and pleasure along the way. It is a gradual buildup of excitement and anticipation, fueled by mutual desire and affection. Each touch, kiss, and caress is imbued with meaning and significance, deepening the bond between partners and intensifying their shared experience.

As partners navigate this journey together, they explore new depths of intimacy and pleasure, discovering hidden desires and unlocking the full potential of their sexual connection. It is a journey marked by spontaneity, creativity, and mutual exploration, where each partner plays an active role in guiding the other towards ultimate satisfaction and fulfillment.

The "Big O" is not merely a physical release, but a moment of transcendence—a culmination of the intense emotional and physical connection between partners. It is a moment of pure ecstasy, where time seems to stand still and the boundaries between self and other dissolve. In this moment, partners are fully present with each other, lost in the blissful embrace of mutual pleasure and intimacy.

By embracing sexual intimacy as a holistic journey, partners can cultivate a deeper understanding of themselves and each other, creating intimacy, trust, and love that extends far beyond the bedroom. It is through this shared exploration of desire and pleasure that couples can forge a bond that is truly unbreakable, enriching every aspect of their relationship and journey together.

Sex is a Lifestyle:

Sexual intimacy is not merely an isolated event but a lifestyle—a vibrant way of being that infuses every aspect of our daily lives with passion, pleasure, and connection. It goes beyond the physical act of sex to encompass our attitudes, beliefs, values, and behaviors surrounding sexuality, shaping how we relate to ourselves and others on a profound level.

Embracing sex as a lifestyle means integrating its principles into our daily existence, prioritizing self-care, self-expression, and self-discovery as essential components of our sexual well-being. This holistic approach recognizes that our sexual health and fulfillment are intrinsically linked to our overall physical, emotional, and mental well-being.

At its core, living a sexual lifestyle involves cultivating a deep sense of intimacy and connection with ourselves and our partners. It means being attuned to our own desires and needs, as well as those of our partners, and actively seeking ways to nurture and enhance our sexual connection.

Simple acts of kindness and affection, such as holding hands, sharing intimate conversations, or expressing gratitude for each other, can greatly impact the quality of our sex lives. These seemingly small gestures of love and appreciation create a foundation of trust, intimacy, and emotional connection that lays the groundwork for satisfying and fulfilling sexual encounters.

Moreover, living a sexual lifestyle involves creating an environment of open communication, honesty, and vulnerability in our relationships. It means being willing to express our desires, fantasies, and boundaries openly and without judgment, while also listening attentively to our partners' needs and concerns.

From a more complex perspective, integrating sex as a lifestyle might involve exploring new sexual experiences and fantasies with our partners, experimenting with different techniques or activities to enhance pleasure and arousal, or even seeking guidance from a therapist or sex educator to address any challenges or concerns that may arise.

Ultimately, living a sexual lifestyle is about embracing our sexuality as an integral part of who we are, celebrating its diversity, complexity, and beauty. It is about encouraging a sense of curiosity, adventure, and playfulness in our relationships, and approaching sex with a spirit of openness, exploration, and mutual respect.

By incorporating the principles of passion, pleasure, and connection into our daily lives, we can create a foundation for a healthy, vibrant, and fulfilling sex life—one that enriches not only our intimate relationships but also our overall sense of well-being and vitality.

Also, embracing sexual intimacy as a lifestyle involves cultivating a foundation of accountability, compassion, honesty, respect, self-discipline, empathy, and integrity in our relationships and interactions.

Accountability prompts us to take responsibility for our actions and choices, building trust and reliability with our partners. When we hold ourselves accountable, we acknowledge the impact of our behavior on our relationships and strive to make choices that prioritize the well-being of ourselves and our partners.

Compassion allows us to empathize with our partner's experiences and emotions, creating a deeper sense of connection and understanding. By approaching our interactions with empathy and compassion, we create a supportive environment where vulnerability is met with acceptance and understanding.

Honesty encourages open communication and transparency, creating an environment of trust and authenticity where desires and boundaries can be freely expressed. When we communicate honestly with our partners, we build a foundation of trust that allows for deeper intimacy and connection.

Respect ensures that each partner's autonomy and dignity are honored, creating space for mutual consent and mutual pleasure. When we respect our partner's boundaries, preferences, and needs, we create an environment where both partners feel valued, heard, and understood.

Self-discipline involves making conscious choices that prioritize our sexual health and well-being, whether it's practicing safe sex, prioritizing self-care, or setting boundaries that align with our values and desires. When we exercise self-discipline in our sexual interactions, we create a foundation of safety and trust that allows for greater exploration and intimacy.

Empathy enables us to attune to our partner's needs and desires, enhancing intimacy and emotional connection. By actively listening to our partner, validating their experiences, and offering support and understanding, we deepen our bond and create a sense of closeness and intimacy.

Integrity guides us to align our actions with our values, creating a sense of authenticity and trustworthiness in our relationships. When we act with integrity, we demonstrate consistency and reliability, building a foundation of trust that allows for vulnerability and emotional intimacy.

By embodying these principles in our daily lives, we create a nurturing and supportive environment for sexual exploration, growth, and fulfillment. When we approach sexual intimacy as a lifestyle, we honor the complexity and depth of our relationships, enabling connection, pleasure, and mutual satisfaction.

A lifestyle devoid of accountability, compassion, honesty, respect, self-discipline, empathy, and integrity can have detrimental effects on our sex lives and relationships. Without accountability, there may be a lack of responsibility for one's actions, leading to breaches of trust and emotional distance between partners. Without compassion and empathy, there may be a failure to understand and support each other's needs, resulting in feelings of isolation and disconnection.

Honesty is essential for maintaining trust and authenticity in relationships; without it, there may be secrecy or deception, eroding the foundation of intimacy and mutual respect. Respect is crucial for establishing boundaries and consent; without it, there may be a disregard for personal autonomy and emotional safety, leading to feelings of coercion or violation.

Self-discipline is necessary for maintaining sexual health and well-being; without it, there may be risky behaviors or neglect of one's physical and emotional needs, resulting in potential harm or dissatisfaction. Integrity ensures consistency and reliability in our actions; without it, there may be inconsistency or unreliability, causing uncertainty and instability in the relationship.

In essence, a lifestyle devoid of these values can lead to a breakdown of trust, communication, and emotional connection, ultimately undermining the quality and satisfaction of our sex lives. It is through embodying these principles that we create a foundation of mutual respect, understanding, and intimacy, creating a healthy and vibrant sexual relationship with our partners.

Sex is a Language:

Sexual intimacy is indeed a language—a rich way of communication that extends far beyond mere words. It is a dance of touch, a symphony of gestures, and a dialogue of shared experiences that speaks directly to the heart and soul. In this deep language, every caress, every kiss, and every embrace carries with it a message—a message of love, desire, and connection.

In the realm of sexual intimacy, nonverbal communication plays a crucial role in nurturing a healthy and vibrant sex life. From the smallest, seemingly insignificant cues to the most profound and complex ones, these nonverbal signals serve as the building blocks of intimacy and understanding between partners. For example, the gentle stroke of a hand along the back can convey reassurance and tenderness, while a passionate kiss on the lips can express longing and desire.

Through nonverbal cues, partners communicate their desires, preferences, and boundaries, creating a safe and supportive environment for sexual exploration and expression. A subtle shift in body language or a lingering gaze can signal consent and invitation, while a withdrawal or tensing of the body may indicate discomfort or reluctance.

In addition to nonverbal cues, verbal communication also plays a vital role in the language of sexual intimacy. Open and honest dialogue allows partners to express their needs, fantasies, and concerns, creating mutual understanding and respect. By articulating desires and boundaries, couples can navigate potential pitfalls and misunderstandings, ensuring that both partners feel heard, valued, and respected.

For example, discussing fantasies and desires can spark excitement and anticipation, while expressing fears or insecurities can build empathy and support. Verbal communication also allows partners to check in with each other during intimate moments, ensuring that both individuals are comfortable and consenting every step of the way.

The Essence Of Sexual Intimacy

The language of sexual intimacy is a dynamic and ever-evolving expression of love, trust, and connection between partners. By listening to each other's cues, both verbal and nonverbal, and communicating openly and honestly, couples can deepen their intimacy and strengthen their bond, creating a fulfilling and satisfying sex life together. Lack or absence of communication creates room for assumption. When partners do not communicate their concerns and preferences, they will assume what the other partner is thinking, opening a huge room for misinterpreting each other.

However, when we fail to utilize the language of sexual intimacy to our advantage, it can have profound effects on our sex lives and relationships. Without effective communication, both verbal and nonverbal, misunderstandings can arise, leading to tension, frustration, and dissatisfaction. Lack of communication can create a barrier to intimacy, preventing partners from fully understanding each other's desires, needs, and boundaries. This can result in mismatched expectations and unmet needs, leading to feelings of rejection, resentment, and disconnection.

Without clear communication, couples may struggle to navigate issues such as consent, sexual preferences, and boundaries, increasing the risk of coercion, pressure, and even trauma. Failure to communicate openly and honestly can also contribute to misunderstandings and misinterpretations, leading to hurt feelings and damaged trust. Moreover, when partners fail to communicate effectively, it can lead to a breakdown in emotional intimacy, further eroding the foundation of the relationship. Without the ability to connect on a deeper level, couples may find themselves feeling disconnected and distant, both inside and outside the bedroom.

In the absence of effective communication, couples may resort to unhealthy coping mechanisms such as avoidance, passive-aggressiveness, or emotional withdrawal, further exacerbating the problems in the relationship. This can create a cycle of conflict and dissatisfaction that undermines the overall health and vitality of the partnership. Ultimately, the failure to use the language of sexual intimacy to our advantage can have far-reaching consequences for our sex lives and relationships. By prioritizing open and honest communication, both verbal and nonverbal, couples can deepen their intimacy, strengthen their connection, and cultivate a fulfilling and satisfying sex life together.

Ultimately, the language of sexual intimacy is a dynamic and ever-evolving expression of love, trust, and connection between partners. By listening to each other's cues, both verbal and nonverbal, and communicating openly and honestly, couples can deepen their intimacy and strengthen their bond, creating a fulfilling and satisfying sex life together. Most of the time we wonder why things are not working out in the bedroom without realizing that we have missed this aspect of sexual intimacy. Speaking this language fluently will highly increase our chances of reaching and experiencing great orgasms, while our failure to speak this language will result in problems during intimacy.

Sex is a Connection of Two Souls:

At its core, sexual intimacy is a deep merging of two souls—an ethereal merging that goes beyond mere physical interaction and delves into the realm of spiritual connection. It is the intertwining of individual energies, a harmonious blending of essences that creates a powerful force greater than the sum of its parts. This alchemical fusion of sexual energy ignites a profound transformation within us, as we surrender to the divine flow of love and passion.

In the sacred space of sexual connection, we are transported to a realm where time ceases to exist, and we are fully present with each other in the eternal now. Here, we experience a deep sense of union with our partner, as our energies intertwine and dance in perfect harmony. Boundaries dissolve, and we are enveloped in a cocoon of blissful surrender, where we are free to express our truest selves without fear or inhibition.

The Essence Of Sexual Intimacy

As we embrace the sacredness of sexual intimacy, we recognize the divine spark that resides within each of us and honor it in our partner. We approach each other with reverence and awe, mindful of the profound gift of love and connection that we share. In this sacred exchange, we become vessels of divine grace, channeling the universal energy of creation through our bodies and souls.

In the dance of intimacy, we bear witness to the beauty and mystery of existence, as we surrender to the divine flow of life force energy that courses through us. We are reminded of the sacredness of all things and the interconnectedness of all beings, as we merge with our partner in a cosmic symphony of love and ecstasy.

In the embrace of sexual intimacy, we are invited to transcend the limitations of the physical world and tap into the boundless reservoir of spiritual energy that resides within us. Here, we discover the true essence of our being—the infinite wellspring of love, passion, and divine connection that lies at the core of our existence.

In the realm of intimacy, distinctions between "I" and "you" dissolve into the indefinable unity of "us." Boundaries blur and identities merge as we lose ourselves in the sacred dance of connection. In this divine union, the lines that separate us fade away, leaving only the pure essence of our shared being. We become intertwined in a realm of love and passion, each thread indistinguishable from the other, until we are no longer two separate entities but one unified whole.

In this state of oneness, time loses its grip, and we are suspended in the eternal moment of now, where past, present, and future converge into a single point of infinite possibility. It is here, in the depths of intimacy, that we discover the true nature of existence—that we are not merely individuals traversing separate paths, but interconnected souls journeying together towards the divine.

While the potential for profound oneness in intimacy is inherent, there are factors that can obstruct its realization, leaving intimacy devoid of meaning and depth. One such barrier is the lack of vulnerability and authenticity between partners. When individuals withhold their true selves out of fear or insecurity, intimacy becomes superficial, and genuine connection remains elusive. Without the courage to reveal our innermost thoughts, feelings, and desires, we erect barriers that prevent true intimacy from blossoming.

Additionally, unresolved conflicts and emotional wounds can hinder the flow of intimacy, creating a sense of distance and disconnection between partners. When past hurts linger unresolved, they cast a shadow over the present moment, obscuring the potential for deep connection and mutual understanding. Without addressing these underlying issues, intimacy becomes marred by tension and mistrust, rendering it hollow and meaningless.

Moreover, the relentless pursuit of physical pleasure at the expense of emotional connection can also thwart the development of true intimacy. When partners prioritize self-gratification over mutual respect and understanding, intimacy devolves into mere physical transactions devoid of emotional resonance. Without the foundation of emotional intimacy, physical encounters lack depth and significance, leaving both partners unfulfilled and disconnected.

Furthermore, external distractions and preoccupations can detract from the present moment, preventing partners from fully immersing themselves in the experience of intimacy. When attention is divided and focus is scattered, intimacy becomes fragmented, and the profound sense of connection is lost amidst the noise of daily life. Without the space for undivided presence and attention, intimacy loses its potency and meaning, reducing it to a short lived moment rather than a transformative experience.

The Essence Of Sexual Intimacy

In essence, when barriers such as lack of vulnerability, unresolved conflicts, prioritization of physical pleasure over emotional connection, and external distractions obstruct the flow of intimacy, it becomes shallow and devoid of meaning. Without the depth of genuine connection and mutual understanding, intimacy loses its transformative power, leaving both partners yearning for a deeper, more meaningful connection.

When the journey, language, lifestyle, and connection of two souls converge, they intertwine in the ultimate dance of sexual intimacy—a symphony of passion, vulnerability, and deep connection. This dance begins with the recognition that sexual intimacy is not merely a physical act but a holistic journey that encompasses the mind, body, and soul.

As partners embark on this journey together, they communicate not only through words but also through the language of touch, gestures, and shared experiences. Through this intimate dialogue, they express their deepest desires, fears, and vulnerabilities, creating a safe space for mutual exploration and discovery.

Furthermore, sexual intimacy becomes a lifestyle—a way of being and relating to one another that permeates every aspect of their lives. They prioritize self-care, authenticity, and mutual respect, recognizing that their sexual health and fulfillment are integral to their overall well-being. This lifestyle builds a culture of trust, openness, and vulnerability, laying the foundation for deep connection and intimacy.

In the dance of sexual intimacy, partners merge their energies and become attuned to each other's needs and desires. They honor the divine spark within themselves and their partners, approaching each other with reverence and gratitude. As they surrender to the moment, boundaries dissolve, and they experience a profound sense of oneness and connection.

This ultimate dance of sexual intimacy is a celebration of love, passion, and connection—a sacred union where souls merge and hearts intertwine.

It is a manifestation of the transformative power of intimacy and the beauty of human connection. As partners embrace this dance with open hearts and minds, they unlock the full potential of sexual intimacy, experiencing joy, fulfillment, and profound connection beyond measure.

Chapter Seven

Exploring Male and Female Psychology in Sexual Intimacy

"The cycle of seeking sexual pleasure with no intention of emotional investment often leads to a never-ending quest for fulfillment that remains perpetually unmet."

Exploring Male And Female Psychology In Sexual Intimacy

Welcome to Chapter Seven of our journey into the realm of sexual intimacy. Here, we're delving into the fascinating world of human psychology, specifically focusing on how men and women perceive and experience intimacy differently.

As a relationship coach rather than a professional psychologist, I'll be approaching this topic from a practical standpoint, aiming to provide insights that are accessible and relevant to our everyday lives. While we may not dive into the depths of academic psychology, the insights shared here will paint a clear picture of the fundamental differences between the male and female psyche when it comes to sexual intimacy.

Throughout this chapter, we'll explore how the mind of a man and that of a woman operate within the context of intimate relationships. By understanding these basic psychological differences, we can gain valuable insights into our own behavior and that of our partners, paving the way for deeper connections and more fulfilling relationships.

It's crucial to recognize that the mind is the most sensitive erotic zone for both men and women, and as we explore the male and female sexual psyche, we must bear this in mind. Our thoughts, desires, and emotions influence our experiences of intimacy, shaping the dynamics of our relationships in profound ways. Through understanding and acknowledging these psychological nuances, we can cultivate greater empathy, communication, and intimacy in our relationships, ultimately developing deeper connections and more satisfying sexual experiences.

Gaining insight into how our minds function in relation to sexual intimacy can indeed enhance our experiences and empower us to take control of our sexual lives. When we understand the workings of our own minds, we become better equipped to navigate our desires, preferences, and boundaries, allowing us to communicate more effectively with our partners and advocate for our needs.

Moreover, understanding the complexities of our partner's mind can provide invaluable insight into their desires, fears, and erotic language. By empathizing with their perspective and recognizing the unique ways in which they experience and respond to intimacy, we can create deeper connections and cultivate more fulfilling sexual relationships.

In essence, knowledge is power when it comes to sexual intimacy. By delving into the complexities of our own minds and those of our partners, we gain a deeper understanding of ourselves and each other, paving the way for more enriching and satisfying sexual experiences.

So, let's embark on this exploration of the human mind and its role in sexual intimacy, keeping in mind that while we may not cover every nuance, the insights shared here will offer valuable perspectives for enhancing our understanding and appreciation of one another.

Our perception of sexual intimacy plays a crucial role in shaping our experience. Our minds act as powerful filters through which we interpret and respond to intimate encounters. The way we view and approach sexual intimacy can either enhance or hinder our enjoyment and fulfillment.

Think about it: if we perceive sexual intimacy as burdensome or negative, our minds may generate feelings of anxiety, stress, or discomfort during intimate moments. Consequently, our bodies react to these mental cues, manifesting physical responses that mirror our mental state. This can result in decreased arousal, difficulty in achieving satisfaction, or even avoidance of intimate situations altogether.

Conversely, when we view sexual intimacy as enjoyable, fulfilling, and natural, our minds can create a positive and conducive environment for intimacy. This positive mindset can lead to increased arousal, heightened pleasure, and deeper connections with our partners.

The phenomenon of sexual tension further illustrates the interplay between the mind and body in shaping our intimate experiences. When we experience sexual tension, whether it's the fluttery feeling in our stomachs when talking to someone we're attracted to or the anticipation leading up to intimate moments, it's our minds creating a heightened state of awareness and arousal. Our bodies respond to the psychological tension we feel, amplifying our physical sensations and enhancing our overall experience of intimacy.

In essence, our perception of sexual intimacy acts as a lens through which we experience and navigate our intimate relationships. By cultivating a positive and open mindset towards intimacy, we can harness the power of our minds to enrich our sexual experiences and deepen our connections with our partners.

Sfiso's Infidelity

Let's dive into the complex relationship between Sfiso and Mahlatse, two young people trying to figure out love and commitment. Sfiso, who's 26, and Mahlatse, 24, have been through a lot together in the two years they've been together. Like any couple, they've had their ups and downs, times of happiness, and moments of sadness.

But things got really tough when Sfiso started getting involved with other women. It hurt Mahlatse deeply because she had given her heart to him completely. His actions broke the trust they had built over time. Feeling lost and betrayed, Mahlatse turned to me, a relationship coach, hoping to find a way to fix what was broken.

Mahlatse's decision to seek help shows how much she believed in their love story. Even though she's hurting, she's not ready to give up just yet. She's holding on to hope and is determined to try everything she can to make things right before calling it quits. This moment is her last chance to save their relationship, showing just how strong her love for Sfiso truly is.

Mahlatse, a petite woman with stunning dark skin, radiates a true African beauty with her curvy figure, thick thighs, and a generous, healthy backside. Despite her physical allure, her most captivating trait lies in her loving and devoted nature, particularly evident in her relationship with Sfiso. Having endured the pain of betrayal in her previous relationship, where her partner cheated on her, Mahlatse made the courageous decision to walk away after investing three years into a love that ultimately proved false.

In contrast, Sfiso stands as an average-height African man, characterized by his gentle demeanor and kindness towards others. His journey into love was marked by a past relationship where he experienced heartbreak, as his partner left him for someone with greater financial means. This betrayal left Sfiso grappling with feelings of inadequacy and loss, shaping his approach to future relationships and influencing the dynamics of his connection with Mahlatse.

As a relationship coach, delving into the backgrounds of Sfiso and Mahlatse revealed some intriguing insights. Despite Sfiso's apparent commitment in his previous relationship, further investigation uncovered a sobering truth: his affection for Mahlatse was rooted not in genuine love, but rather in a physical attraction. It became evident that Mahlatse's physical features bore a striking resemblance to those of Sfiso's ex-girlfriend, igniting a subconscious desire within him to fill the void left by his former partner.

It became clear that Sfiso's heart still harbored unresolved feelings for his ex, and Mahlatse unwittingly became a surrogate for the woman he could not forget. His expectations of experiencing the same level of sexual satisfaction with Mahlatse as he had with his ex-girlfriend were shattered, as their encounters failed to measure up to his nostalgic memories. This revelation shed light on the underlying complexities of their relationship, where unmet expectations and unresolved emotions threatened to unravel the fragile bond between them.

Exploring Male And Female Psychology In Sexual Intimacy

Witnessing Mahlatse's profound emotional investment in the relationship, I couldn't help but feel a deep sense of empathy for her dilemma. It was evident that she had poured her heart and soul into their partnership, only to be met with betrayal and heartbreak. As I delved deeper into Sfiso's patterns of infidelity, a troubling pattern emerged: his pursuit of sexual gratification seemed to overshadow any genuine commitment to Mahlatse.

In my role as a relationship coach, I've encountered similar scenarios before, where individuals like Sfiso seek short lived pleasure without regard for the emotional consequences. It became apparent that Sfiso was unlikely to leave Mahlatse for another woman; instead, he would be content to engage in extramarital affairs while maintaining the facade of commitment; this is common. He would even go to an extend of doing everything to keep his relationship with her, but men like him seldom repent from their infidelity. His behaviour of jumping from one pleasure spot to another perpetuated a cycle of dissatisfaction and unfulfilled expectations.

The cycle of seeking sexual pleasure with no intention of emotional investment often leads to a never-ending quest for fulfillment that remains perpetually unmet. Despite Sfiso's efforts to find satisfaction elsewhere, the reality is that his search for short lived pleasure will only leave him trapped in a cycle of dissatisfaction and emotional emptiness. For Mahlatse, the challenge lies in confronting this painful truth and finding the strength to break free and walk away from this dilemma.

Let me show you how this pattern often perpetuate itself in certain men.

Excessive Pleasure-Seeking

In my first book, "The Paradigms of Love," I touched on the subject of excessive love for sex, driven by a fixation on the "Big O." In this phenomenon, women become objects of pleasure rather than individuals with their own desires and emotions. Every woman he encounters is perceived as a potential source of gratification—a pleasure spot to fulfill his desires without regard for her humanity.

Driven by fantasies and idealized perceptions of sexual fulfillment, the man pursues one pleasure spot after another in search of that moment of pleasure. In his mind, he has already envisioned the kind of pleasure he will have with each woman he meets.

However, reality often fails his expectations. Despite his initial excitement and anticipation of the pleasure he would have with these women, the actual experience leaves him feeling empty and unsatisfied. Disappointed by the difference between anticipation and reality, he finds himself restless and discontent.

Faced with disappointment, the man is driven to seek out new pleasure spots in a relentless pursuit of satisfaction. Each encounter reinforces the belief that fulfillment lies just out of reach, perpetuating a never-ending cycle of seeking.

This continual search for satisfaction becomes self-perpetuating, trapping the man in a destructive pattern of dissatisfaction and emotional emptiness. Despite the futility of his efforts, he remains unable to break free from the cycle, driven by an insatiable desire for the pleasure he craves. His hunger for satisfaction becomes impossible to satisfy; it's like pouring water into a bucket with a hole in it—no matter what you do, your efforts to fill it with water will go to waste.

The Real Problem

The problem lies not in the mere enjoyment of sexual experiences, which is a natural and healthy aspect of human intimacy, but rather in the excessive fixation on achieving the 'Big O'—the orgasm—as the sole measure of satisfaction and fulfillment. This excessive preoccupation with the physical climax can overshadow the deeper emotional and psychological aspects of intimacy.

To truly understand the significance of this, we must recognize that the shackles of this fixation first bind the mind before they manifest in our actions. It's not merely a matter of physical behavior but rather the psychological landscape within which our sexual selves reside.

Psychology plays a profound role in shaping our sexual experiences and behaviors. Our thoughts, beliefs, and emotions deeply influence how we perceive and respond to intimate encounters. When our focus becomes solely fixated on achieving the physical climax, we neglect the richness of emotional connection, intimacy, and vulnerability that truly defines fulfilling sexual experiences.

Moreover, this excessive emphasis on the 'Big O' can lead to a disconnect between mind and body, where pleasure becomes detached from genuine intimacy. It perpetuates a cycle of seeking instant gratification without addressing deeper emotional needs or creating genuine connections with our partners.

Breaking free from these psychological shackles requires a shift in mindset—a reevaluation of what truly brings fulfillment and satisfaction in our sexual lives. It entails recognizing the importance of emotional connection, communication, and mutual respect in manifesting truly enriching and satisfying sexual experiences.

By acknowledging the role of psychology in our sexual selves, we empower ourselves to transcend the limitations of mere physical gratification and embrace a more holistic and fulfilling approach to intimacy. It's through this deeper understanding and appreciation of the psychological nuances of our sexual experiences that we can truly unlock the untapped potential of sexual intimacy.

Sfiso's Infidelity (Continued)

Indeed, uncovering the underlying complexities of Sfiso's behavior sheds light on the deeper psychological dynamics at play within their relationship. Sfiso's dissatisfaction with his sex life with Mahlatse reveals a deeper longing for his past relationship and an inability to fully invest himself in their current partnership.

The realization that Sfiso was seeking his ex in Mahlatse highlights the complexities of unresolved emotions and unmet needs within intimate relationships. Despite Mahlatse's unwavering loyalty and dedication, she could never fulfill the role of Sfiso's ex-girlfriend. This painful truth is something Mahlatse must come to terms with as she grapples with the harsh reality of her partner's emotional unavailability.

Sfiso's sudden venture into infidelity serves as a clear sign that as long as he has not healed from his failed relationship with his ex, no one else will satisfy him. Not only could Mahlatse not fully satisfy Sfiso, but his actions underline the depth of his unresolved emotional turmoil.

As a relationship coach, guiding Sfiso to understand himself and his motivations is crucial in archiving personal growth and healing. By helping him confront his own insecurities and desires, Sfiso can begin to untangle the complexities of his emotional landscape and embark on a journey towards self-discovery and fulfillment.

However, the road to healing is fraught with challenges, and Mahlatse must also confront her own feelings of betrayal and disappointment. Recognizing that she cannot build a future with Sfiso on a foundation of broken trust and unmet expectations is a painful but necessary step towards her own healing and empowerment.

Ultimately, both Sfiso and Mahlatse must embark on individual journeys of self-discovery and healing before they can hope to rebuild their relationship on a stronger and more authentic foundation. It is a journey filled with uncertainty and pain, but also one that offers the possibility of growth, forgiveness, and ultimately, true fulfillment.

In essence, what this reveals is that true sexual satisfaction goes beyond physical acts alone; it resides in the realm of the mind. Until Sfiso confronts and resolves his emotional baggage, he will continue to seek fulfillment in short-lived pleasures, leaving a void that no physical encounter can ever fill.

Likewise, Mahlatse must recognize that her own fulfillment cannot be reliant upon Sfiso's validation or affection. True satisfaction begins within, and until both partners find peace and contentment within themselves, they will remain trapped in a cycle of chasing unattainable desires and short-lived pleasures, forever elusive like chasing the wind.

The core psychological differences between men and women's sexual behavior

When delving into the core psychological differences between men and women's sexual behavior, it's essential to recognize that these differences often stem from a combination of biological, social, and cultural factors. Here's an exploration of some key distinctions:

Biological Factors: Biological variances between men and women, such as hormonal differences, can significantly influence sexual behavior. For instance, men typically have higher levels of testosterone, which is associated with increased libido and sexual desire. Women, on the other hand, experience hormonal fluctuations throughout their menstrual cycle, affecting their sexual arousal and interest.

Emotional Connection: Generally, women tend to place greater emphasis on emotional connection and intimacy in sexual relationships compared to men. For many women, feeling emotionally connected to their partner is crucial for experiencing sexual satisfaction. In contrast, men may prioritize physical attraction and sexual compatibility, although emotional connection remains important for many.

Communication Styles: Men and women often have different communication styles when it comes to expressing their sexual needs and desires. Women may prefer indirect communication and rely on non-verbal cues to convey their desires, while men may be more direct and explicit in expressing their sexual preferences.

Sexual Response: Research suggests that men and women may have different patterns of sexual response. While men typically have a linear model of sexual response, progressing from arousal to orgasm, women's sexual response is often more complex and variable. Factors such as context, emotional state, and relationship dynamics can significantly impact women's sexual arousal and satisfaction.

Sexual Motivations: Men and women may have different motivations for engaging in sexual activity. While men may be more driven by physical pleasure and the pursuit of sexual gratification, women's motivations may be influenced by factors such as emotional intimacy, relationship satisfaction, and the desire for connection.

Perception of Sexuality: Cultural and societal norms often shape individuals' perceptions of sexuality differently based on gender. Men may be socialized to prioritize sexual conquests and demonstrate virility, while women may face societal expectations regarding sexual modesty and purity. These societal influences can impact how men and women navigate their sexual identities and behaviors.

Overall, understanding these core psychological differences can provide valuable insights into the complexities of male and female sexual behavior. By acknowledging and respecting these differences, individuals can establish healthier and more fulfilling sexual relationships.

Female Sexual Psyche

This reflection brings to light the importance of understanding and appreciating the complexities of the female psyche in the context of sexual intimacy. Dr. Laurie Mintz's statement underscores the notion that the quality of a sexual experience is not solely determined by physical attributes, such as penis size, but rather by the emotional connection and mutual respect between partners.

Indeed, the female psyche encompasses a wide range of emotions, desires, and preferences that may differ from those of men. Recognizing and honoring these differences is essential for creating meaningful and satisfying sexual relationships. Women may prioritize emotional intimacy, communication, and mutual pleasure over physical attributes alone.

It is crucial for men to recognize that women's sexual experiences are influenced by a multitude of factors, including their emotional state, past experiences, and individual preferences. Understanding and respecting these factors can lead to deeper connections and more fulfilling sexual encounters.

Furthermore, this reflection highlights the importance of self-awareness and self-understanding for women themselves. By understanding their own desires, boundaries, and needs, women can advocate for their own pleasure and satisfaction in sexual encounters. Empowering women to explore and embrace their sexuality is essential for promoting sexual health and well-being.

The state of a woman's psyche plays a pivotal role in shaping her sexual experiences within a relationship. When a woman feels emotionally secure, valued, and respected by her partner, it creates an environment conducive to intimacy and pleasure. Factors such as peace of mind, confidence in her partner, and effective communication contribute to her overall sense of well-being and satisfaction.

Moreover, the way a man interacts with his partner can profoundly impact her sexual experience. Small gestures of affection, such as buying flowers or speaking her erotic language fluently, can enhance emotional intimacy and deepen the connection between partners. By understanding and responding to her needs and desires, a man can create an atmosphere of trust and mutual respect, building a more fulfilling sexual relationship.

However, external factors such as anxiety, insecurity, and fear of sexually transmitted infections (STIs) can negatively impact a woman's sexual experience. These anxieties can create barriers to intimacy and pleasure, hindering her ability to fully engage in sexual activity.

Furthermore, a woman's attitude towards sex, shaped by cultural, societal, and personal beliefs, can influence her sexual experiences. Negative or degrading views of sex can lead to feelings of shame, guilt, or discomfort, making it difficult for her to enjoy sexual encounters fully.

During one of my pastoral duties, I had a conversation with a young woman who was a university student at the time. In the course of our discussion, I complimented her by telling her that she was beautiful. However, to my surprise, she vehemently denied my compliment, insisting that she was not beautiful at all.

Intrigued by her response, I delved deeper into the conversation, hoping to understand her perspective better. Eventually, she opened up and revealed to me that her grandmother had consistently told her throughout her life that she was ugly. Shockingly, her grandmother's intention behind these hurtful remarks was to protect her granddaughter from the attention of boys. She believed that by convincing her granddaughter that she was unattractive, she could deter her from associating too closely with boys, thus safeguarding her innocence.

This was eye-opening and deeply concerning. It highlighted the profound impact that external influences, especially those from trusted family members, can have on a person's self-perception and self-esteem. In this case, the young woman's grandmother's misguided attempts to protect her had inadvertently instilled feelings of inadequacy and self-doubt, ultimately affecting her confidence and how she viewed herself.

This anecdote serves as a touching reminder of the importance of promoting positive self-image and challenging harmful beliefs that undermine individuals' sense of self-worth. It underscores the need for sensitivity and empathy in addressing the psychological factors that can impact a woman's sexual experiences and overall well-being.

Addressing these underlying psychological issues is crucial for promoting sexual health and well-being in women. By challenging negative beliefs, building self-confidence, and promoting positive body image, individuals can create a supportive and empowering environment for women to explore and embrace their sexuality.

In essence, sexual intimacy for women is a holistic experience that encompasses the mind, body, and spirit. Unlike men, whose arousal may be predominantly physical, women often require a deeper emotional connection and psychological comfort to fully engage in and enjoy sexual encounters. This means that factors such as trust, emotional intimacy, and a sense of security play pivotal roles in a woman's sexual experience.

By prioritizing emotional connection, communication, and mutual respect, couples can cultivate more fulfilling and satisfying sexual relationships. When partners take the time to understand each other's needs, desires, and boundaries, they can create a safe and nurturing environment where both individuals feel valued and empowered.

In such relationships, intimacy is not just about physical pleasure but also about emotional connection and mutual fulfillment. Ultimately, creating a deeper understanding and appreciation of the complex interplay between the mind, body, and spirit in women's sexual experiences can lead to more profound and meaningful connections between partners, enriching their relationships in profound ways.

Exploring Male And Female Psychology In Sexual Intimacy

Male Sexual Psyche

The societal indoctrination of young boys into patriarchal norms begins at a tender age, perpetuating a cycle of toxic masculinity and sexualization. From childhood, boys are taught to believe in their superiority over girls, creating a mindset of dominance and entitlement. This ingrained belief system places immense pressure on boys to perform, both sexually and in all aspects of life, reinforcing the idea that masculinity is synonymous with power and control.

As boys grow up, these societal expectations continue to shape their attitudes and behaviors, leading to a distorted perception of masculinity and relationships. In many cultures, the number of girlfriends a man has is often equated with his status and masculinity, promoting a shallow and transactional view of relationships devoid of commitment and connection.

Unfortunately, society often fails to recognize the detrimental impact of this indoctrination on the mental and emotional well-being of boys. The pressure to conform to rigid gender roles and expectations can result in deep-seated insecurities, anxiety, and a distorted sense of self-worth. Moreover, the emphasis on sexual prowess and dominance can manifest in harmful behaviors, both in and out of the bedroom.

Society often finds itself shocked and dismayed when adult men exhibit behaviors akin to social thugs and terrorists within the realm of sexual intimacy. Yet, what many fail to recognize is that this phenomenon is not born out of a vacuum; rather, it is the culmination of societal norms, expectations, and cultural conditioning that have groomed these individuals. They are taught to suppress emotions, equating vulnerability with weakness, and encouraged to assert power and control in all aspects of their lives.

This distorted view of masculinity not only harms their partners but also restricts their own emotional growth. It leads to a disregard for the emotional well-being of their partners and a prioritization of their own desires and ego. In the minds of these individuals, the concept of commitment becomes foreign and even threatening. They have been conditioned to believe that true masculinity lies in their ability to 'lead the pack' and indulge in a lifestyle of promiscuity.

However, as society evolves, there's a growing recognition of the need for a new breed of men – those who are not defined by outdated notions of masculinity but rather embrace empathy, vulnerability, and emotional intelligence. These 'soft men' are the heralds of change, willing to challenge traditional gender roles and embrace norms and traditions that are relevant to today's lifestyle.

Encouraging soft masculinity is crucial in this endeavor. Soft men understand that true strength lies not in dominance or control, but in vulnerability and emotional openness. They prioritize communication and mutual respect in their relationships, valuing the emotional well-being of their partners as much as their own.

Society's glorification of the 'alpha male' archetype perpetuates harmful behaviors, but it's time to redefine what it means to be a man. It's time to celebrate sensitivity, compassion, and empathy – traits that are often sidelined in traditional notions of masculinity.

It is essential for society to recognize its role in perpetuating these harmful ideologies and to work towards dismantling them. This requires a collective effort to challenge traditional gender roles, promote healthy expressions of masculinity, and create environments where emotional vulnerability and empathy are valued.

Addressing the root causes of these behaviors is crucial in creating a society where sexual intimacy is characterized by mutual respect, understanding, and genuine connection, rather than domination and exploitation. Let us strive to create a world where soft masculinity thrives, and all individuals are free to express themselves authentically and empathetically.

Lastly, the male sexual psyche is deeply influenced by societal norms, expectations, and cultural conditioning, which often perpetuate harmful ideologies of toxic masculinity. From a young age, boys are indoctrinated into patriarchal beliefs, creating a mindset of dominance and entitlement. This distorted perception of masculinity not only impacts their relationships but also contributes to emotional turmoil and harmful behaviors.

However, there is hope for change. As society evolves, there's a growing recognition of the need for a new paradigm of masculinity—one that embraces empathy, vulnerability, and emotional intelligence. Soft masculinity, characterized by sensitivity, compassion, and respect, offers a path forward.

Encouraging soft masculinity requires a concerted effort to challenge traditional gender roles and promote healthy expressions of masculinity. It's time to redefine what it means to be a man and celebrate traits that have long been sidelined in favor of dominance and control.

By creating environments where emotional vulnerability and empathy are valued, we can dismantle harmful ideologies and create a society where sexual intimacy is characterized by mutual respect, understanding, and genuine connection. Let us work together to cultivate a culture of empathy and compassion, where both men and women can thrive in relationships built on equality and mutual respect.

Sexual Intimacy in Relationships in the 21st Century

In the 21st century, sexual intimacy in relationships has undergone significant transformations, largely influenced by societal changes and the digital age. One notable shift is the monetization of love and sex, where aspects of romantic relationships are increasingly commodified and commercialized.

This is evident in a prevailing culture where women often prioritize their partners' financial status over other qualities, sometimes sacrificing emotional fulfillment for financial security. They may choose to stay with partners who provide financial stability, even if they are emotionally absent or abusive. This commercialization of love and relationships not only undermines the essence of genuine connection but also contributes significantly to the rising divorce rates. Ultimately, the pursuit of financial security over emotional fulfillment perpetuates a cycle of dissatisfaction and unfulfillment in modern relationships.

Another notable difference in relationships today is that more and more women would rather live single lives instead of spending a lifetime with men who do not value commitment. They choose rather to have children out of wedlocks and raise them by themselves, and there is so little tolerance for patriarchy.

Simultaneously, the escalating divorce rate reflects deeper societal issues surrounding the perception of relationships and commitment. In an era where instant gratification is prioritized and disposable culture is normalized, the value of long-term commitment and emotional connection in relationships is often overlooked. This lack of commitment is exacerbated by societal pressures, unrealistic expectations perpetuated by media, and the glorification of individualism over partnership.

The pervasive influence of social media and digital communication further complicates matters, creating a false sense of intimacy while diminishing genuine human connection. Couples may struggle to maintain authentic, meaningful relationships amidst the constant distractions and temptations of the online world.

As a result, sexual intimacy within relationships is often affected, with partners feeling disconnected or unsatisfied. The pursuit of better sex or new sexual experiences becomes a common theme, leading some individuals to seek fulfillment outside of their primary relationships. The ease of access to alternative sexual partners through dating apps or online platforms exacerbates the temptation to stray.

Moreover, the normalization of infidelity in popular culture and media further undermines the sanctity of committed relationships, perpetuating a cycle of mistrust and betrayal. Partners may rationalize their extramarital affairs as a means of seeking sexual satisfaction or emotional fulfillment that they perceive as lacking in their primary relationship.

In conclusion, the landscape of sexual intimacy in relationships in the 21st century is deeply intertwined with complex psychological dynamics. The monetization of love and sex, coupled with societal pressures and technological advancements, has reshaped the way individuals perceive and experience intimacy.

At the heart of these changes lies a fundamental need for genuine human connection and emotional fulfillment. Despite the prevalence of digital communication and instant gratification, true intimacy requires a deeper understanding of oneself and one's partner. It demands vulnerability, empathy, and a willingness to prioritize the needs and desires of each other.

In navigating the challenges of modern relationships, it is essential to recognize the psychological factors at play and actively work towards building genuine connection and mutual respect. By cultivating open communication, creating emotional intimacy, and prioritizing commitment over convenience, couples can create a foundation for fulfilling and satisfying sexual relationships in the 21st century.

Chapter Eight

Exploring Male and Female Sexual Physiology

"Sexual intimacy is a two-way street where prioritizing each other's pleasure and well-being is important."

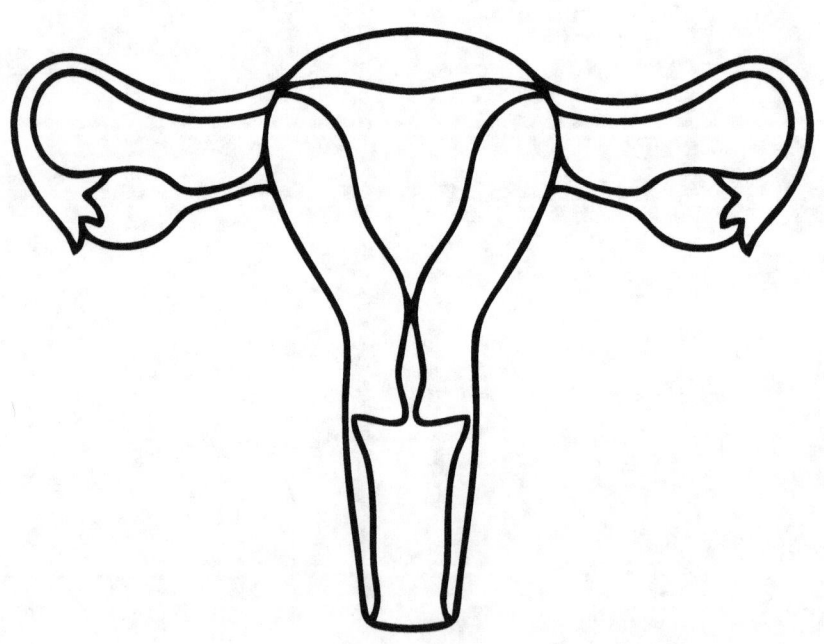

Exploring Male And Female Physiology In Sexual Intimacy

In this chapter, we are diving into the interesting and rather complex world of male and female sexual physiology. From the perspective of a relationship coach rather than a scientist, our aim is to shed light on these matters in a way that is accessible and relevant to everyday relationships.

One of the obvious issues in relationships today is the lack of understanding between men and women about each other's bodies and desires. Even more concerning is the fact that many individuals, both men and women, have limited knowledge about their own bodies and sexual functions.

Amidst all the topics we've covered so far, this chapter stands out as one of the most crucial. Understanding the physiological aspects of sexual intimacy lays the foundation for fulfilling and satisfying experiences in relationships.

Throughout this chapter, we'll explore various aspects of human physiology, with a particular focus on female sexual physiology. Topics will include sexual organs, the female menstrual cycle, and more. So, get ready to embark on this journey through the complexities of human sexual physiology.

In our exploration of male and female sexual physiology, it's crucial to acknowledge the evolving dynamics of sexual orientation, particularly among women. In recent years, there has been a notable trend where many women identify as bisexual rather than exclusively heterosexual. This shift can be attributed to various factors, one of the most significant being the changing understanding of sexual orientation.

One contributing factor to this trend is the realization that women do not necessarily require penile penetration for satisfying sexual intercourse. Surprisingly, research suggests that approximately 80% of women do not reach orgasm through penile penetration alone. This revelation challenges the conventional notion that a man's penis size is associated with sexual satisfaction for women. This realization can be unsettling for men who have been conditioned to believe that physical attributes dictate sexual prowess.

In light of this, many women opt to explore relationships with other women, recognizing that they may have a better chance of experiencing fulfilling sexual encounters. Women understand the intricacies of the female body and are often more attuned to their partner's needs and desires. As a result, they may be more skilled at providing pleasurable sexual experiences compared to men.

Understanding and embracing the diversity and complexity of women's sexual responses and preferences is essential for creating fulfilling and satisfying sexual relationships, irrespective of gender or sexual orientation.

This recognition underscores the importance of both partners comprehending each other's physiological needs and preferences. While women benefit from understanding men's physiology to satisfy them, men also need to grasp women's physiology for mutual satisfaction.

Sexual intimacy is a two-way street where prioritizing each other's pleasure and well-being is important. Effective communication plays a central role in achieving this mutual satisfaction, allowing partners to tailor their sexual interactions to each other's unique desires and preferences.

Even if someone has access to resources like "The Untapped World of Sexual Intimacy" and reads chapters on male and female sexual physiology, human beings are inherently complex individuals with unique desires and preferences. While general knowledge can provide a foundation, true sexual satisfaction often requires a deeper understanding of your partner's specific needs and desires.

Encouraging open and honest communication about sexual preferences, boundaries, and desires is key to a fulfilling sexual relationship. Partners should feel comfortable discussing what feels good, what doesn't, and any fantasies or desires they may have. By actively listening to each other and being receptive to feedback, couples can enhance their sexual experiences and deepen their connection.

Ultimately, prioritizing communication allows partners to tailor their sexual interactions to each other's unique preferences and create a mutually satisfying and fulfilling sexual experience.

Sexual Organs

Before delving into the intricate details of male and female sexual anatomy, it's crucial to grasp the fundamental dual purpose of sexual organs: reproduction and pleasure. While some organs are primarily designed for reproduction, others are specialized for the experience of sexual pleasure. However, it's important to recognize that all these organs work in harmony during sexual encounters, facilitating both reproduction and pleasure.

Throughout our exploration of sexual anatomy, you'll notice how certain organs are dedicated solely to pleasure, such as the clitoris in females and the glans penis in males. Conversely, organs like the testes and ovaries are primarily responsible for producing gametes (sperm and eggs) for reproduction. Despite these distinctions, each organ contributes to the overall sexual experience, creating a complex interplay of physiological responses and sensations.

By understanding the dual nature of sexual organs – serving both reproductive and pleasurable functions – we gain insight into the intricacies of human sexual physiology. This foundational knowledge sets the stage for a comprehensive exploration of male and female sexual anatomy, shedding light on their roles in sexual arousal, intercourse, and reproductive processes.

Let us now turn our focus to the details of sexual organs. We will delve into both male and female sexual anatomy, clarifying their differences, similarities, functions, and natural designs.

Male Sexual Anatomy:

The male sexual anatomy is characterized by several distinct organs, each playing a vital role in the process of sexual arousal and reproduction.

Penis

Perhaps the most recognizable male sexual organ, the penis serves dual functions in sexual intercourse and urination. Structurally, it consists of three cylindrical columns of erectile tissue, which become engorged with blood during sexual arousal, resulting in erection. The glans penis, located at the tip, is highly sensitive to stimulation, facilitating sexual pleasure.

It's also worth noting that the tissues comprising the glans penis are analogous to those found in the clitoris, underscoring the sensitivity of this region for both men and women. For women seeking to understand the level of sensitivity of the glans, they can draw parallels to the highly sensitive nature of the clitoris.

In uncircumcised men, the glans penis is typically covered by a foreskin, providing protection and maintaining its sensitivity. Conversely, in circumcised men, the glans is exposed, devoid of the protective foreskin covering. This anatomical distinction can influence sexual experiences and sensations for individuals of different circumcision statuses.

Testes (Testicles)

In men, the testes, also known as testicles, serve as essential glands for reproductive and hormonal functions. They are responsible for two primary functions: sperm production and testosterone secretion.

Sperm Production: Within the testes, specialized structures called seminiferous tubules produce sperm through a process known as spermatogenesis. Sperm production is vital for male fertility and reproduction.

Testosterone Production: The Leydig cells, located in the testes, produce testosterone, the primary male sex hormone. Testosterone plays a crucial role in regulating various bodily functions, including the development of secondary sexual characteristics such as facial hair, deep voice, and muscle mass. Additionally, testosterone influences libido or sexual desire in men.

In women, although they do not have testes like men, they still produce small amounts of testosterone primarily from the ovaries and adrenal glands. However, the levels of testosterone in women are significantly lower compared to men.

Impact on Sexual Intimacy: Testosterone plays a significant role in sexual desire and arousal for both men and women. In men, adequate testosterone levels are necessary for maintaining libido and erectile function. Conversely, in women, testosterone contributes to sexual desire, sensitivity to sexual stimuli, and overall sexual satisfaction. Imbalances in testosterone levels can affect sexual intimacy in both men and women, leading to changes in libido, arousal difficulties, and sexual dysfunction. Therefore, maintaining hormonal balance, including optimal testosterone levels, is essential for healthy sexual functioning and intimacy in relationships.

Scrotum

The scrotum, often referred to colloquially as the "ball sack," is a unique anatomical structure found in males. It serves several essential functions related to the health and function of the testes, as well as playing a role in sexual intercourse.

Anatomy and Composition: The scrotum is a pouch of skin and underlying muscle located underneath the penis. It is divided into two compartments, each containing one testis. The skin of the scrotum is unique in its texture and thickness, providing protection to the testes while allowing for flexibility and movement. Within the scrotum, there are also layers of connective tissue, blood vessels, nerves, and the cremaster muscle, which help regulate the position and temperature of the testes.

Temperature Regulation: One of the primary functions of the scrotum is to regulate the temperature of the testes. Sperm production, or spermatogenesis, is highly sensitive to temperature changes. Therefore, the scrotum serves as a natural thermostat, adjusting the position of the testes in response to environmental temperature changes. When it's cold, the scrotum contracts, bringing the testes closer to the body to maintain warmth. Conversely, in warmer temperatures, the scrotum relaxes and hangs lower, allowing the testes to cool down.

Sensitivity to Sexual Stimulation: The scrotum contains numerous nerve endings and sensory receptors, making it highly sensitive to touch and sexual stimulation. Many men find that stimulation of the scrotum, either through touch, licking, or gentle massaging, enhances sexual arousal and pleasure during sexual activity. The degree of sensitivity can vary from person to person, but for many men, the scrotum plays a significant role in sexual enjoyment and orgasm.

During sexual intercourse, the scrotum often contracts and moves closer to the body in response to sexual arousal and impending ejaculation. This motion helps elevate the testes and tighten the scrotal sac, providing additional stimulation to the penis and enhancing the sensations experienced during ejaculation. Additionally, some sexual positions may involve direct contact or pressure on the scrotum, further enhancing sexual pleasure for both partners.

Exploring Male And Female Physiology In Sexual Intimacy

It is worth noting that while the scrotum is a unique male structure, there are some similarities with certain female genital organs. For example, the labia majora in women, which are the outer folds of skin surrounding the vaginal opening, bear some resemblance to the scrotum in terms of their protective function and sensitivity to touch. Like the scrotum, the labia majora contain nerve endings and sensory receptors that contribute to sexual arousal and pleasure in women.

In summary, the scrotum is a specialized anatomical structure designed to protect and regulate the temperature of the testes while also contributing to sexual pleasure and arousal in men. Its sensitivity to sexual stimulation and role in sexual intercourse highlight its importance in male sexual physiology and intimate experiences.

Male Sexual Anatomy:

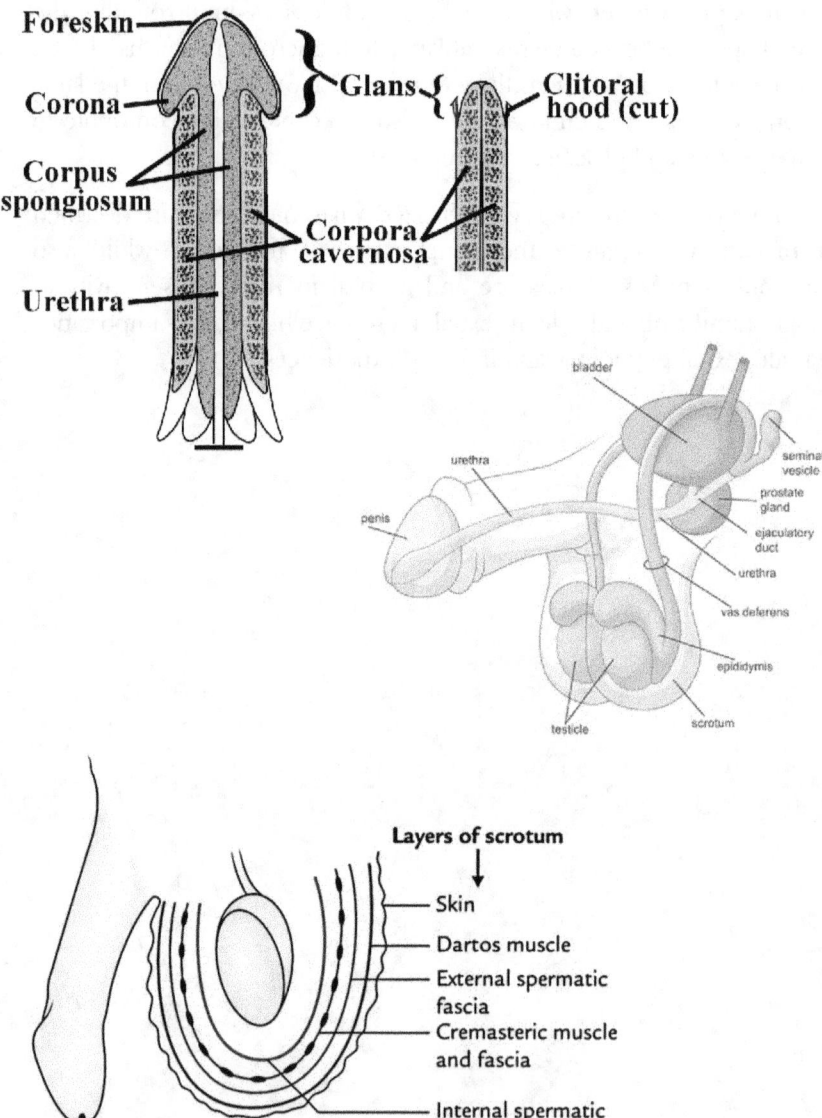

Female Sexual Anatomy:

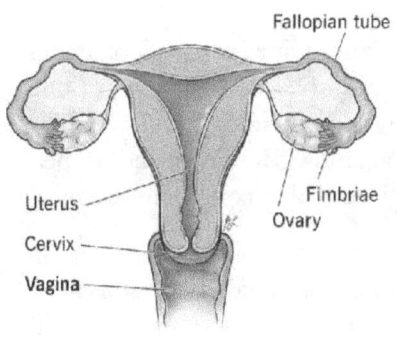

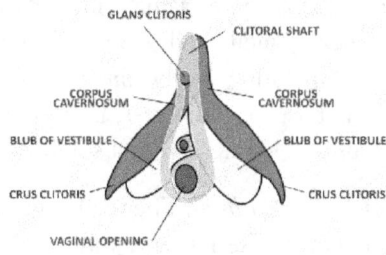

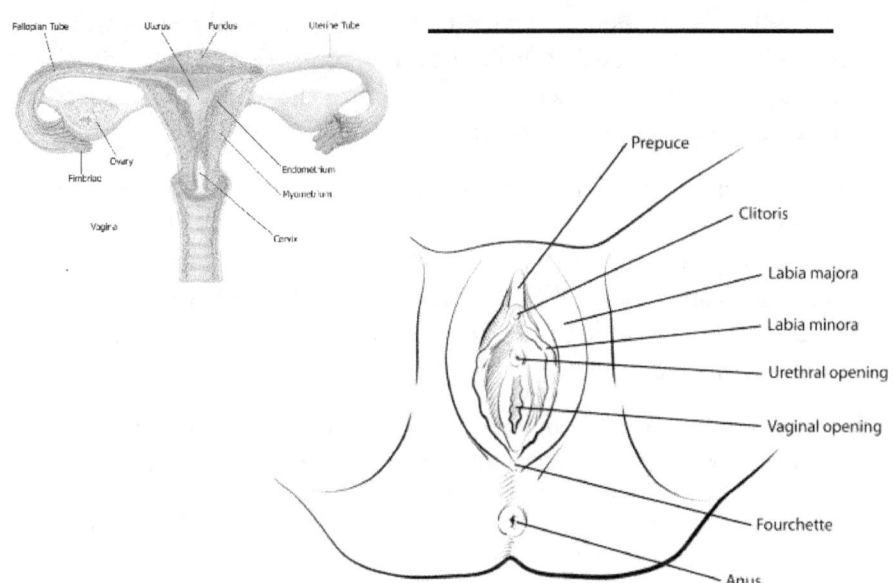

Female Sexual Anatomy:

The female sexual anatomy is equally complex, consisting of organs specialized for reproduction and sexual pleasure.

Vagina

The vagina is often misunderstood as the primary sexual organ in women. However, it's essential to recognize that the vagina is just one component of a woman's sexual anatomy and physiology, similar to how the penis is just one part of male sexual anatomy. Both men and women have multiple erogenous zones and structures that contribute to sexual pleasure and arousal.

Muscular Canal: The vagina is indeed a muscular canal that extends from the external genitals (vulva) to the cervix of the uterus. It serves several functions, including as the birth canal during childbirth and facilitating sexual intercourse. However, it's important to note that sexual pleasure and arousal in women are not solely dependent on vaginal penetration.

Rich in Nerve Endings: The vaginal walls are rich in nerve endings, much like the penis, clitoris, and other erogenous zones in both men and women. These nerve endings contribute to sexual arousal and pleasure when stimulated through touch, pressure, or friction during sexual activity. Therefore, it's inaccurate to prioritize the vagina as the sole source of sexual pleasure for women.

While vaginal penetration is one aspect of sexual intercourse, it's essential to recognize that it's not the sole determinant of sexual satisfaction for women. Many women derive pleasure from clitoral stimulation, external genital stimulation, and other erogenous zones during sexual activity. Therefore, sexual satisfaction in women is multifaceted and not limited to vaginal penetration alone.

In summary, the vagina is an integral part of a woman's sexual anatomy and physiology, but it's not the sole or primary sexual organ. Women, like men, have multiple erogenous zones and structures that contribute to sexual pleasure and arousal. Understanding and appreciating the complexity of female sexual anatomy is crucial for promoting sexual health, satisfaction, and intimacy in relationships.

Clitoris

Often regarded as the female counterpart to the penis, the clitoris is a highly sensitive organ located at the top of the vulva, beneath the clitoral hood. Its structure and function make it a crucial component of female sexual anatomy and physiology.

Sensitivity and Pleasure: The clitoris is dedicated solely to sexual pleasure, containing thousands of nerve endings that respond to stimulation. Its sensitivity is comparable to that of the male glans (penis head), making it a primary source of sexual pleasure for many women. Stimulation of the clitoris can elicit intense sensations of pleasure and arousal, leading to orgasm in some cases.

Analogous Structure to the Male Glans: In terms of structure and function, the clitoris bears similarities to the male glans (penis head). Both organs are highly sensitive and densely innervated, making them focal points for sexual stimulation and pleasure. Additionally, like the male glans, the clitoris becomes engorged with blood during sexual arousal, enhancing sensitivity and responsiveness to touch.

Complex Anatomy: While the visible portion of the clitoris is relatively small, it extends internally, with roots and erectile tissue that can contribute to sexual arousal and pleasure. The clitoris consists of a glans, which is the exposed portion located beneath the clitoral hood, as well as two shafts (crura) and bulbs that extend internally. This complex structure allows for a variety of sensations and responses to different types of stimulation.

Role in Sexual Intimacy: The clitoris plays a central role in female sexual arousal and pleasure. Stimulation of the clitoris, whether through direct touch, oral stimulation, or other means, can lead to heightened arousal, lubrication, and ultimately, orgasm for many women. Understanding the anatomy and sensitivity of the clitoris is essential for promoting sexual satisfaction and intimacy in relationships.

In summary, the clitoris is a highly sensitive and erotically charged organ that serves as a primary source of sexual pleasure for many women. Its structure and function are analogous to the male glans, highlighting the similarities in sexual anatomy and physiology between men and women. Recognizing the importance of clitoral stimulation in sexual intimacy is crucial for enhancing sexual satisfaction and promoting healthy, fulfilling relationships.

Uterus

The uterus, also known as the womb, is a unique reproductive organ found exclusively in females. It plays a pivotal role in the reproductive process, serving as the site for embryo implantation, fetal development during pregnancy, and labor during childbirth. While the uterus is primarily associated with reproduction, it can indirectly influence sexual intimacy in several ways:

Reproductive Function: The main function of the uterus is to provide a nurturing environment for the developing fetus during pregnancy. After conception, a fertilized egg travels down the fallopian tubes and implants itself into the uterine lining. The uterus then undergoes significant changes to support the growing embryo and fetus throughout pregnancy, including supplying nutrients, oxygen, and protection.

Menstrual Cycle: The uterus is also involved in the menstrual cycle, which is a natural process that occurs in women of reproductive age. Each month, the inner lining of the uterus, known as the endometrium, thickens in preparation for potential pregnancy. If pregnancy does not occur, the endometrium is shed during menstruation, resulting in menstrual bleeding. We will discuss these in much detail later.

Sexual Intimacy: While the uterus is not directly involved in sexual arousal or pleasure, its position and size can influence sexual intercourse to some extent. During sexual arousal, the uterus may lift slightly, allowing for easier penetration of the vagina. Additionally, some individuals may experience uterine contractions or spasms during orgasm, which can contribute to sensations of pleasure.

For some individuals, the uterus may hold symbolic significance in sexual intimacy, representing fertility, femininity, or motherhood. However, its role in sexual pleasure is indirect, as most sensations of pleasure during intercourse are derived from stimulation of the clitoris, vagina, and other erogenous zones.

In summary, while the uterus is essential for reproductive function and pregnancy, its direct role in sexual intimacy is limited. However, its presence and function can indirectly influence sexual experiences through its impact on reproductive health, menstrual cycles, and psychological factors related to femininity and fertility.

Ovaries

The ovaries are a pair of small, almond-shaped organs situated on either side of the uterus within the female reproductive system. They play crucial roles in female reproduction and hormone regulation. Here's a closer look at their functions and significance in sexual physiology:

Egg Production (Oogenesis): One of the primary functions of the ovaries is to produce eggs, or ova, through a process called oogenesis. During fetal development, the ovaries contain millions of immature egg cells called oocytes. However, only a fraction of these oocytes will mature and be released during a woman's reproductive years. Each month, typically starting around puberty and continuing until menopause, one mature egg is released from one of the ovaries in a process known as ovulation. If fertilization occurs, the egg may be fertilized by sperm and develop into a pregnancy.

Hormone Production: In addition to egg production, the ovaries are responsible for synthesizing and secreting female sex hormones, primarily estrogen and progesterone. These hormones play critical roles in regulating the menstrual cycle, supporting reproductive health, and influencing secondary sexual characteristics. Estrogen, in particular, is essential for maintaining the health of the reproductive organs, promoting the development of secondary sexual characteristics during puberty, and regulating the menstrual cycle. Progesterone helps prepare the uterus for pregnancy and supports early pregnancy if fertilization occurs.

Menstrual Cycle Regulation: The ovaries are central to the regulation of the menstrual cycle, which is the monthly process that prepares the female body for potential pregnancy. Throughout the menstrual cycle, the ovaries release hormones that stimulate the growth and maturation of follicles, which contain developing egg cells. Ovulation occurs when a mature egg is released from a ruptured follicle into the fallopian tube, where it may be fertilized by sperm. If fertilization does not occur, hormone levels decline, triggering the shedding of the uterine lining during menstruation.

While the ovaries are not directly involved in sexual arousal or pleasure, their hormonal activities influence reproductive health, sexual desire, and overall well-being. Balanced hormone levels, particularly estrogen and progesterone, are essential for maintaining sexual function, vaginal lubrication, and the health of reproductive tissues. Imbalances or disruptions in ovarian function, such as polycystic ovary syndrome (PCOS) or ovarian cysts, can affect fertility and sexual health.

In summary, the ovaries play integral roles in female reproduction, hormone regulation, and menstrual cycle regulation. While they are not directly involved in sexual arousal or pleasure, their functions have profound effects on reproductive health, sexual function, and overall well-being. Understanding the role of the ovaries is essential for comprehending female sexual physiology and reproductive health.

While the male and female sexual organs exhibit distinct anatomical features, they share a common purpose in facilitating sexual pleasure and reproduction. Understanding the functions and structures of these organs is essential for comprehending the complexities of human sexual physiology.

Exploring Erogenous Zones: Unveiling the Pleasure Spots

In the realm of sexual intimacy, erogenous zones play a pivotal role in igniting arousal and enhancing pleasure. These sensitive areas of the body are rich in nerve endings, making them particularly responsive to tactile stimulation. While some erogenous zones are well-known and commonly explored, others remain overlooked or neglected. Let's embark on a journey through these pleasure spots, uncovering both the familiar and the often underestimated:

Common Erogenous Zones

Lips and Mouth: Kissing and oral stimulation of the lips and mouth can elicit intense pleasure and arousal due to the abundance of nerve endings in these areas.

Neck and Nape: Gentle kissing, nibbling, or light caresses along the neck and nape can be highly arousing, as these areas are sensitive to touch and proximity to the ears.

Breasts and Nipples: For many individuals, breast and nipple stimulation is highly arousing and can lead to heightened pleasure and orgasm. Varying degrees of pressure and touch can evoke different sensations.

Genitalia: The genitals, including the clitoris, penis, scrotum, and perineum, are classic erogenous zones rich in nerve endings. Direct stimulation of these areas can induce sexual arousal and pleasure.

Overlooked Erogenous Zones

Ears: The ears contain numerous nerve endings and can be incredibly sensitive to light touches, kisses, or whispers. Gentle nibbling or sucking on the earlobes can also be highly arousing.

Inner Thighs: The inner thighs are often overlooked but can be highly sensitive to touch. Light caresses or kisses along the inner thighs can build anticipation and arousal.

Lower Back: The lower back is an erogenous zone that can be particularly responsive to gentle strokes, massages, or kisses. It's an area that can evoke pleasurable sensations when stimulated.

Feet: Feet contain numerous nerve endings and can be highly sensitive to touch. Foot massages, kisses, or gentle caresses can be surprisingly arousing for some individuals.

Cultural and Personal Variations

It's important to note that individuals may have unique preferences and sensitivities when it comes to erogenous zones. Cultural influences, personal experiences, and individual anatomy can all shape an individual's response to different types of stimulation. What may be highly pleasurable for one person may not necessarily elicit the same response in another.

Investing time in exploring erogenous zones before venturing into genital stimulation can greatly enhance sexual pleasure and intimacy. By focusing on these pleasure spots, partners can build anticipation, increase arousal, and deepen their connection. Additionally, exploring erogenous zones allows for the discovery of new sources of pleasure and can lead to more varied and satisfying sexual experiences.

In conclusion, understanding and exploring erogenous zones can enhance sexual intimacy and pleasure in relationships. By paying attention to both familiar and overlooked pleasure spots, partners can discover new ways to arouse and satisfy each other, creating deeper connections and more fulfilling sexual experiences.

Sex hormones and their contribution in sexual intimacy

Let's delve into the interplay of sex hormones in both men and women and how they contribute to sexual intimacy:

In Men:

Testosterone: Testosterone is the primary male sex hormone produced mainly in the testes. It plays a central role in regulating libido, or sexual desire, as well as erectile function and sperm production. Higher levels of testosterone are generally associated with increased sexual arousal and motivation for sexual activity.

Estrogen: While estrogen is typically considered a female sex hormone, men also produce small amounts of estrogen. In men, estrogen helps regulate libido and erectile function, and it also plays a role in maintaining bone density and cardiovascular health. However, estrogen levels in men are significantly lower than in women.

In Women:

Estrogen: Estrogen is the primary female sex hormone produced mainly in the ovaries. It plays a crucial role in regulating the menstrual cycle, promoting the development of secondary sexual characteristics, and maintaining reproductive health. Estrogen also influences sexual desire and arousal by increasing blood flow to the genitals and promoting vaginal lubrication.

Progesterone: Progesterone is another important female sex hormone produced primarily in the ovaries. It plays a key role in preparing the uterus for pregnancy and regulating the menstrual cycle. Progesterone levels fluctuate throughout the menstrual cycle, peaking during the luteal phase (the second half of the cycle). While progesterone itself does not directly affect sexual desire, it can influence mood and overall well-being, which may indirectly impact libido.

Testosterone: Although testosterone is often associated with male sexuality, women also produce small amounts of testosterone in the ovaries and adrenal glands. Testosterone contributes to women's libido, sexual arousal, and sensitivity to sexual stimuli. While women have lower testosterone levels compared to men, fluctuations in testosterone levels throughout the menstrual cycle can influence sexual desire and responsiveness.

Interplay in Sexual Intimacy:

In both men and women, the interplay of sex hormones is crucial for sexual intimacy. Testosterone, estrogen, and progesterone all contribute to libido, sexual arousal, and overall sexual function. Fluctuations in hormone levels throughout the menstrual cycle can influence sexual desire and responsiveness, with peak fertility typically occurring around ovulation when estrogen levels are highest.

Additionally, hormonal changes associated with aging, pregnancy, menopause, and medical conditions can impact sexual function in both men and women. Understanding the role of sex hormones and their interplay in sexual intimacy can help individuals navigate changes in their sexual health and maintain satisfying and fulfilling sexual relationships.

Exploring Female Menstrual Circle

Understanding the menstrual cycle is indeed crucial for both men and women when it comes to sexual intimacy and overall relationship dynamics. The differences in hormonal profiles between men and women, with men having higher testosterone levels while women undergo cyclical hormonal changes, highlight the unique aspects of female sexual physiology.

For men, the consistent presence of testosterone contributes to a relatively stable sexual desire. However, women experience fluctuations in hormones throughout their menstrual cycle, which can significantly impact their sexual desire, arousal, and responsiveness. These hormonal shifts affect not only physical sensations but also mood and emotional states, which can influence sexual intimacy within relationships.

Men who are attuned to their partner's menstrual cycle can better understand and support them through the various phases. They can adjust their approach to sexual initiation and intimacy based on their partner's hormonal fluctuations, optimizing the timing for deeper connection and pleasure. Moreover, being aware of these hormonal changes cultivates empathy and communication within the relationship, enhancing overall intimacy and satisfaction.

Recognizing the significance of the menstrual cycle in sexual dynamics underscores the importance of education and open dialogue between partners. By embracing this aspect of female physiology, couples can navigate sexual intimacy with greater sensitivity, responsiveness, and mutual satisfaction.

The menstrual cycle consists of four distinct phases, each characterized by hormonal changes and physiological events. Let's explore each phase in detail:

1. Menstrual Phase (Days 1-5):

- The menstrual phase marks the beginning of the menstrual cycle and typically lasts from day 1 to day 5.

- During this phase, the uterine lining, known as the endometrium, sheds in response to a decrease in estrogen and progesterone levels.
- Menstrual bleeding occurs as the unfertilized egg, along with the endometrial tissue, is expelled through the vagina.
- Women may experience symptoms such as menstrual cramps, bloating, and fatigue during this phase.
- During the menstrual phase, when estrogen and progesterone levels are low, some women may experience decreased sexual desire.
- Menstrual symptoms such as cramps, bloating, and fatigue may also affect mood and emotional well-being, potentially reducing interest in sexual activity.

However, individual experiences vary, and some women may find that sexual activity helps alleviate menstrual discomfort or improves mood.

Safety: Engaging in sexual activity during menstruation is generally safe, although some individuals may prefer to avoid it due to personal comfort or hygiene reasons.

Considerations: The risk of pregnancy is typically low during menstruation, but it's still possible, especially if a woman has a shorter menstrual cycle. Protection against sexually transmitted infections (STIs) should still be prioritized.

Consequences: Intercourse during menstruation may lead to increased risk of bacterial infections due to the presence of menstrual blood. Some individuals may also experience discomfort or pain during sex due to menstrual cramps or sensitivity. The use of condom is highly advised if you are to engage sexually during this time.

2. Follicular Phase (Days 1-13):

- The follicular phase begins on the first day of menstruation and extends until ovulation, typically lasting from day 1 to day 13 of the menstrual cycle.
- During this phase, follicle-stimulating hormone (FSH) stimulates the growth and development of ovarian follicles, each containing an immature egg.
- Estrogen levels gradually increase, leading to the thickening of the endometrium in preparation for potential implantation of a fertilized egg.
- Ovulation usually occurs around the midpoint of the follicular phase, triggered by a surge in luteinizing hormone (LH).
- As estrogen levels gradually rise during the follicular phase, many women experience an increase in sexual desire and arousal.
- Heightened energy levels and a sense of well-being during this phase may contribute to a greater interest in sexual activity.
- Emotional responses during the follicular phase may be more positive and optimistic, reflecting the influence of rising estrogen levels on mood.

Safety: The follicular phase, leading up to ovulation, is generally considered a safe time for sexual activity. However, it's important to use contraception if pregnancy is not desired.

Considerations: Ovulation can sometimes occur earlier or later than expected, so relying solely on calendar-based methods for contraception may not be reliable.

Consequences: If contraception is not used and ovulation occurs earlier than expected, there may be a risk of unintended pregnancy.

3. Ovulatory Phase (Day 14):

- The ovulatory phase is a brief period centered around ovulation, typically occurring on day 14 of the menstrual cycle.
- Ovulation is the release of a mature egg from the dominant ovarian follicle into the fallopian tube, where it may be fertilized by sperm.
- Estrogen levels peak just before ovulation, stimulating the release of LH, which triggers the rupture of the mature follicle and the release of the egg.
- Women may experience changes in cervical mucus consistency and increased sexual desire during this phase, making it an optimal time for conception.
- The ovulatory phase, characterized by peak estrogen levels just before ovulation, often coincides with a surge in sexual desire and libido.
- Many women report feeling more sexually receptive and responsive during this phase, making it an optimal time for intimacy and conception.
- Emotional responses may also be enhanced, with some women experiencing heightened feelings of attractiveness and confidence.

Safety: The ovulatory phase is the most fertile time in the menstrual cycle, with the highest chance of conception. If pregnancy is desired, this is an optimal time for sexual activity without contraception.

Considerations: For individuals trying to conceive, tracking ovulation using methods such as ovulation predictor kits or basal body temperature charting can help identify the most fertile days.

Consequences: Engaging in unprotected sex during the ovulatory phase significantly increases the risk of pregnancy. However, for those not wishing to conceive, it's essential to use contraception effectively.

Exploring Male And Female Physiology In Sexual Intimacy

4. Luteal Phase (Days 15-28):

- The luteal phase begins immediately after ovulation and lasts until the start of the next menstrual period, typically spanning from day 15 to day 28 of the menstrual cycle.
- Following ovulation, the ruptured follicle transforms into a structure called the corpus luteum, which secretes progesterone to prepare the endometrium for potential implantation of a fertilized egg.
- Progesterone levels increase, reaching their peak around mid-luteal phase, to maintain the thickened endometrial lining and support early pregnancy.
- If fertilization does not occur, progesterone levels decline towards the end of the luteal phase, triggering the shedding of the endometrium and the onset of menstruation.
- During the luteal phase, progesterone levels increase, which may lead to fluctuations in sexual desire and emotional responses.
- Some women may continue to experience heightened sexual desire early in the luteal phase, while others may notice a decline as progesterone levels rise.
- Emotional changes during the luteal phase may include mood swings, irritability, or heightened sensitivity, commonly referred to as premenstrual syndrome (PMS).

Safety: Sexual activity during the luteal phase is generally safe, but precautions should still be taken to prevent unintended pregnancy and STIs.

Considerations: While the risk of pregnancy is lower during the luteal phase compared to the ovulatory phase, it's still possible, especially if a woman has a shorter menstrual cycle.

Consequences: Unprotected sex during the luteal phase may result in unintended pregnancy if ovulation occurs earlier than expected.

Additionally, concerns such as **PMS** symptoms or discomfort may affect sexual enjoyment.

Sexual desire and emotional responses can fluctuate throughout the menstrual cycle, influenced by hormonal changes and other factors. However, open communication and understanding between partners can help navigate these fluctuations and maintain intimacy and connection.

Understanding the four phases of the menstrual cycle—menstrual, follicular, ovulatory, and luteal—provides valuable insight into fertility, reproductive health, and hormonal fluctuations that impact a woman's overall well-being. By recognizing these changes, individuals can make informed decisions about sexual activity and contraception.

Effective communication between partners about desires, preferences, and contraceptive needs is crucial for maintaining a healthy and satisfying sexual relationship while minimizing risks. This mutual understanding builds trust, respect, and support, enhancing overall intimacy and strengthening the bond between partners.

Impact of Contraceptives on Sexual Desire and Intimacy:

1. Hormonal Contraceptives (e.g., Birth Control Pills, Patch, Ring):

- Hormonal contraceptives contain synthetic hormones (estrogen and/or progestin) that mimic the natural hormones in a woman's body to prevent pregnancy.
- Some women report changes in sexual desire while using hormonal contraceptives. While some may experience an increase in libido due to stabilized hormone levels, others may notice a decrease in sexual desire as a side effect of the contraceptive.
- Mood swings, decreased vaginal lubrication, or changes in orgasm intensity are some potential side effects that can impact sexual intimacy for some individuals.

- However, for others, the peace of mind provided by effective contraception can enhance sexual intimacy by reducing anxiety about unintended pregnancy.

2. Non-Hormonal Contraceptives (e.g., Condoms, Diaphragms, Copper IUD):

Non-hormonal contraceptives, such as condoms and copper intrauterine devices (IUDs), do not affect hormone levels in the body.

Condoms, while primarily used as a barrier method to prevent pregnancy and STIs, can also impact sexual intimacy by altering sensation for both partners. Some individuals may find condoms reduce sensitivity, while others may prefer the added reassurance they provide.

Copper IUDs work by releasing copper ions that are toxic to sperm, preventing fertilization. While they do not affect hormonal balance, some women may experience heavier periods or increased menstrual cramps, which can indirectly impact sexual intimacy.

Impact of Hormonal Contraceptives on Hormonal Regulation:

1. Estrogen and Progestin Combination Contraceptives:

- Estrogen and progestin combination contraceptives, such as birth control pills, patches, and rings, work by inhibiting ovulation, thickening cervical mucus to prevent sperm from reaching the egg, and thinning the uterine lining to prevent implantation.
- These contraceptives can affect the natural hormonal fluctuations of the menstrual cycle, leading to more stable hormone levels. While this can provide benefits like reduced menstrual cramps and more predictable periods, it may also impact libido and sexual responsiveness for some individuals.

2. Progestin-Only Contraceptives (e.g., Mini-Pill, Depo-Provera Shot, Implant):

- Progestin-only contraceptives primarily work by thickening cervical mucus and thinning the uterine lining to prevent pregnancy. They may also suppress ovulation in some cases.
- While progestin-only contraceptives generally have fewer side effects compared to combination contraceptives, some users may experience changes in libido, mood swings, or irregular bleeding, which can affect sexual desire and intimacy.

Navigating Contraceptive Choices and Sexual Health:

- Choosing the right contraceptive method involves considering individual preferences, medical history, lifestyle factors, and relationship dynamics.
- Open communication between partners about contraceptive needs, sexual desires, and any changes experienced while using contraceptives is essential for maintaining intimacy and mutual satisfaction.
- Regular check-ins with healthcare providers can help address concerns, adjust contraceptive methods if needed, and ensure overall sexual health and well-being.

Understanding how different contraceptives impact sexual desires, hormonal regulation, and overall sexual intimacy is crucial for individuals and couples to make informed decisions that align with their needs and preferences. The choice of contraceptive should not be an individual decision, as it will affect both partners.

When it comes to choosing a contraceptive method, individuals benefit from educating themselves about the available options. This includes understanding how each method works, its efficacy rates, potential side effects, and how it may influence their sexual health and intimacy. Factors such as lifestyle, medical history, relationship dynamics, and future reproductive goals should also be considered in this decision-making process.

It's important to acknowledge that different contraceptives can affect sexual desires and intimacy in various ways. For example, hormonal contraceptives like birth control pills, patches, and injections can alter estrogen and progestin levels in the body, potentially impacting mood, energy levels, and sexual function. Couples should be prepared to discuss openly any changes they experience in libido, sexual responsiveness, or overall satisfaction, and work together to address concerns or make adjustments to their contraceptive strategy.

Establishing open communication within the relationship is essential for creating a supportive environment where contraceptive preferences, concerns, and experiences can be openly discussed. Mutual support involves actively listening to each other's perspectives, validating feelings and experiences, and collaborating on finding solutions that prioritize both partners' well-being. Seeking guidance from healthcare providers or sexual health professionals can provide additional support and resources to address contraceptive-related issues and optimize sexual health outcomes.

Flexibility and adaptability are also important when it comes to contraceptive decision-making. Recognizing that contraceptive needs and preferences may change over time allows couples to remain open to exploring different options and adjusting their approach as needed to maintain a fulfilling and satisfying sexual relationship.

Ultimately, by approaching contraceptive decision-making with openness, communication, and mutual support, individuals and couples can navigate the complexities of sexual health while prioritizing their overall well-being and relationship satisfaction. Embracing a collaborative and adaptable mindset creates resilience and strengthens the foundation of intimacy and connection within the partnership.

Chapter Nine

The Art Of
Making Love

"Foreplay is a profound exploration of each other's bodies. It is a time to appreciate the unique curves, textures, and sensations that make each partner unique."

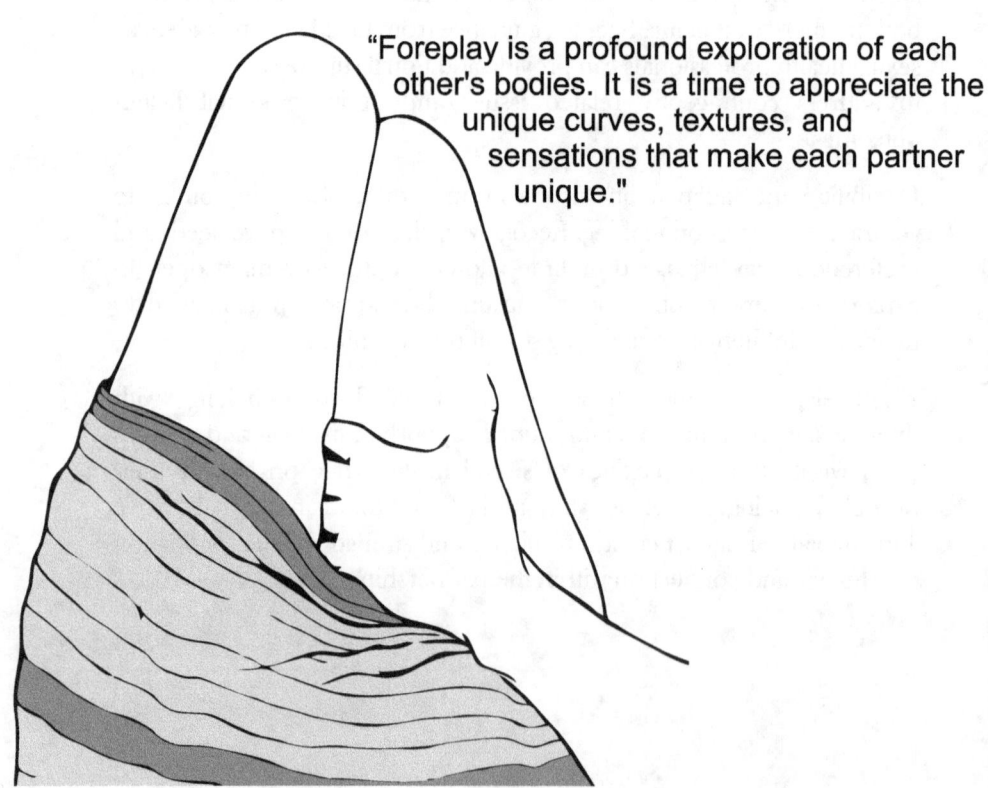

The Art Of Making Love

In this chapter, we embark on a journey that acknowledges the profound impact of the person with whom one engages in intimacy. Beyond techniques and physical attributes, we recognize that the quality of the connection shared with a partner can profoundly shape the entire experience, making it truly memorable.

As we delve into the art of making love, we recognize that one of the most crucial decisions is the choice of a sex partner. It's not merely about finding someone to fulfill physical desires but about seeking a connection that resonates on a deeper level—an emotional and spiritual bond that elevates the act of intimacy to an art form.

In our discussions with individuals, we often encounter concerns that extend beyond technique or performance. In one such instance, a client expressed anxiety about penis size, fearing it might affect his ability to please his partner. In response, I emphasized a fundamental truth: that it is not the size of his manhood that matters the most, rather it is who the person is. He might have the perfect manhood according to your perception, but if he is a jack, the perfectness of his manhood would not change him.

We encourage a shift in focus—from anxieties about physical attributes to cultivating qualities that truly matter in a relationship: empathy, understanding, and genuine connection. By prioritizing emotional intimacy and striving to be the best partner one can be, individuals can nurture a healthier and more satisfying sex life.

Thus, as we navigate the art of making love, we invite you to consider not only the techniques and practices but also the essence of the connection shared with your partner. By embracing authenticity, vulnerability, and a genuine desire to connect, you lay the groundwork for a deeply fulfilling and memorable intimate experience—one that transcends physicality and resonates on a profound emotional level. Welcome to a journey where the true art of making love begins with the choice of a partner and extends to the depths of their heart and soul.

Furthermore, it's important to recognize that many bedroom issues stem not from performance issues, but rather from relational challenges that manifest as barriers to great sex. Miscommunications, unresolved conflicts, and emotional distance can all dampen the flames of passion and hinder intimacy. In these instances, addressing the underlying relational dynamics becomes paramount.

By developing open communication, addressing emotional needs, and nurturing trust and connection outside the bedroom, couples can dismantle these barriers and pave the way for a more satisfying and harmonious sexual relationship. Thus, while technique and physicality certainly play a role, it's often the quality of the relationship and the depth of emotional connection that ultimately determine the richness of the intimate experience.

Let us delve into the relationship between Marcus and Matseleng:

The Story of Marcus & Matseleng: The Conversation

"I can't wait to see you tonight, the day is taking too long to end and all I want is to watch you naked and smell your skin."

Matseleng couldn't help but smile as she read Marcus's message. His message carried a sense of naughtiness and desire, and it stirred her emotions. It had been a while since they first met at Dijong Eatery, the unexpected encounter that had led to their deep connection.

As the memories of that day flooded her mind, she felt some warmth inside her. The way Marcus walked into the eatery with his confident aura, apologizing for being late and yet captivating her attention instantly, was a moment engraved in her memory.

The Art Of Making Love

She got lost in her own world as he spoke, an introverted soul who rarely interacted with strangers, but something about Marcus had drawn her out of her shell. The mix-up with Mrs. Kunene and the way she had invited him to join her table felt like a turning point. It was as if fate had intervened to bring them together.

As she stood there, reminiscing about that day, she couldn't help but appreciate the journey they had embarked upon since then. The shared moments, the laughter, the vulnerabilities they had revealed to each other – all of it had woven a strong bond between them. And now, the playful and intimate texts they exchanged were a proof to their deepening connection.

Matseleng's response, filled with her own playful longing, reflected her comfort and affection for Marcus. It was a beautiful exchange of emotions that showcased their understanding of each other's desires.

"I can't wait for you to come back, I will be barely dressed," she texted back as she succumbed to her playful thoughts.

The clock slowly ticked towards the moment he would be home. Matseleng couldn't help but feel the excitement building up within her. She knew that tonight would be steamy and full of mystery. The anticipation and longing for each other made the day feel even slower.

When Marcus read the text, he recalled the first time his eyes locked with hers; it was that same day at Dijong Eatery. He had expected Mrs. Kunene to be an elderly lady, but he found himself at a table with a young and beautiful woman. At that moment, it didn't occur to him that the woman in front of him was much younger.

She had a dark complexion with big, round, and brownish eyes. She possessed a calm and welcoming demeanor, causing Marcus to feel embarrassed to meet her gaze because he thought she was a married woman. Marcus's confidence was shaken and humbled in front of

Matseleng. He had never been in such a situation before, nor had he ever found himself intimidated by a woman.

It was mostly the aura that Matseleng carried that drew him to her. She was the first woman of color to capture his heart in a manner he had never thought possible.

"I can't wait to look deep into your eyes and see through your soul," he wrote.

Marcus was connected to his emotions, and he knew how to express himself. He often looked at her in the eye and communicated with her soul in ways no one else had ever done. He knew how to read her thoughts, and sometimes it scared her because she felt like he was seeing through her.

At times, Matseleng would shy away from such interactions as she found them overwhelming. Marcus knew how to communicate with her through sheer silence, and this deepened their connection.

When she read the text, she felt naked and vulnerable, sinking deep into an emotional rollercoaster. It was amazing how small things affected her; Matseleng was an emotional wreck, often crying over little gestures.

Lesson Learned:

The exchange between Marcus and Matseleng beautifully illustrates how sexual intimacy begins with who we are as individuals and the depth of connection we share with our partner. Their playful and intimate texts reflect a level of comfort and affection that has been nurtured through shared experiences and open communication.

The build-up to desire, as evidenced by their day-long anticipation, underscores the importance of cultivating desire beyond the physical realm. Their longing for each other extends throughout the day, fueled by playful messages and memories of their initial encounter at Dijong

Eatery. This anticipation heightens their excitement and sets the stage for a steamy and fulfilling night together.

In a healthy relationship, partners create memories that serve to deepen their connection and define their mental state as a couple. Marcus and Matseleng's journey from their first meeting to their intimate exchanges reflects the richness of their shared experiences and the emotional intimacy they've cultivated along the way. These memories not only strengthen their bond but also contribute to their overall mental and emotional well-being as a couple.

However, negative experiences and unresolved issues can disrupt this connection and provoke negative emotions when thinking of one another. Matseleng's vulnerability and emotional fluctuations suggest that unresolved issues or past traumas may be impacting her emotional state. It's essential for Marcus and Matseleng to address these issues openly and compassionately, healing and strengthening their bond even further.

Ultimately, Marcus and Matseleng's exchange serves as a poignant reminder of the transformative power of emotional intimacy in sexual relationships. By nurturing authenticity, vulnerability, and open communication, couples can cultivate a deep and fulfilling connection that transcends the physical and enriches every aspect of their relationship.

Building emotional intimacy is indeed paramount in a relationship, as it forms the foundation upon which all aspects of the partnership, including sexual intimacy, thrive. Couples who prioritize emotional connection often find that their physical relationship flows more naturally, without the struggles commonly associated with the bedroom.

However, creating emotional intimacy goes beyond the realm of mere communication—it's about consistently demonstrating acts of affection and kindness that speak to the unique needs and desires of our partners. Understanding and speaking each other's love languages throughout the day can significantly contribute to this process, as it shows a genuine effort to connect and resonate with our partner's emotions.

The emotions we evoke within our partners through our words, actions, and gestures play a pivotal role in establishing and deepening emotional intimacy. Whether it's a heartfelt compliment, a reassuring touch, or a thoughtful gesture, these expressions of love and appreciation contribute to a sense of closeness and connection between partners.

It's essential to debunk the misconception that certain needs, such as the desire for peace, are exclusive to one gender. Peace is not solely a special need for men—it is a fundamental requirement for the well-being and harmony of both partners in a relationship. Creating a peaceful and nurturing environment where both individuals feel valued, respected, and understood is essential for cultivating emotional intimacy and a thriving partnership.

Building emotional intimacy requires a continuous investment of time, effort, and genuine care from both partners. By prioritizing acts of affection, speaking each other's love languages, and creating a peaceful and supportive environment, couples can lay the groundwork for a deeply fulfilling and mutually satisfying relationship in and out of the bedroom.

The orgasmic experience in emotional intimacy, unlike its physical counterpart, is not short-lived but lingers in the heart for as long as couples continuously nurture and cherish each other with acts of kindness and emotional presence. It is sustained by a consistent flow of affection, empathy, and genuine care between partners, creating a deep sense of security and assurance in the relationship.

This enduring sense of fulfillment arises from the ongoing cultivation of emotional connection and intimacy. As couples consistently demonstrate their love and commitment through acts of kindness, understanding, and support, they reinforce the bonds of trust and affection that underpin their relationship. Each act of kindness serves as a gentle caress to the heart, nurturing the emotional connection and sustaining the orgasmic experience of intimacy.

Moreover, emotional presence plays a crucial role in deepening this experience. When partners are fully present and attentive to each other's needs, desires, and emotions, they create a sacred space where intimacy can flourish. It's about more than just physical proximity—it's about being attuned to each other's innermost thoughts and feelings, sharing in each other's joys and sorrows, and offering unwavering support and understanding.

In this state of emotional intimacy, couples find a profound sense of security and assurance in their relationship. They feel deeply seen, heard, and valued by their partner, knowing that they can rely on each other for comfort, encouragement, and unwavering support. This sense of security acts as a foundation for their relationship, creating a deep sense of trust and mutual respect that strengthens their bond even further.

Ultimately, the orgasmic experience in emotional intimacy is evidence to the transformative power of love, kindness, and emotional connection. It is sustained by a continuous exchange of affection and emotional presence, creating a lasting sense of security and assurance that enriches the relationship and nourishes the souls of both partners.

So, cultivating a lifestyle of kindness, empathy, and consideration lays the foundation for a deeply fulfilling and intimate relationship. It's the small gestures of love and thoughtfulness that create the depth of intimacy and connection between partners.

Whether it's surprising each other with gifts like flowers or gadgets, writing love letters, or leaving random love notes in unexpected places, these acts of affection show a genuine effort to cherish and appreciate one another. They serve as reminders of the love and admiration shared between partners, strengthening the bonds of affection and deepening emotional intimacy.

Moreover, making living together an exciting journey involves infusing everyday life with moments of joy, spontaneity, and adventure. It's about finding beauty and wonder in the ordinary, and approaching each day with a sense of curiosity and enthusiasm. From exploring new hobbies together to embarking on spontaneous outings, couples can create a sense of excitement and anticipation that keeps their relationship vibrant and alive.

By embracing a lifestyle of love, kindness, and adventure, couples can nurture a relationship that thrives on mutual respect, understanding, and appreciation. It's about prioritizing each other's happiness and well-being, and celebrating the unique bond that unites them as partners on this beautiful journey called life.

The Story Of Marcus And Matseleng: Vulnerability

"I can't wait to look deep into your eyes and see through your soul," he wrote.

Marcus was connected to his emotions, and he knew how to express himself. He often looked at her in the eye and communicated with her soul in ways no one else had ever done. He knew how to read her thoughts, and sometimes it scared her because she felt like he was seeing through her.

At times, Matseleng would shy away from such interactions as she found them overwhelming. Marcus knew how to communicate with her through sheer silence, and this deepened their connection.

When she read the text, she felt naked and vulnerable, sinking deep into an emotional rollercoaster. It was amazing how small things affected her; Matseleng was such an emotional wreck, often crying over little gestures.

She was still wearing her towel from the shower, and she felt as if he was watching her. Though she felt vulnerable, she also felt safe, allowing herself to be absorbed by him. Sometimes, due to her childhood traumas, she would close up to him in fear of victimization, but Marcus made it easier for her to overcome her fears.

"Sometimes you send chills to my spine," she expressed her feeling of vulnerability.

Matseleng was sexually molested at the age of 9 by one of the respected members of her family. The incident had always made her to flee from any situation that made her feel vulnerable. Sometimes during her intimate moment with Marcus she would withdraw into a shell and just grow cold.

Initially, Marcus struggled to comprehend Matseleng's reactions stemming from her past trauma. However, over time, they engaged in open conversations about her fears and triggers, leading to better understanding between them. When she confided in him about the chills she experienced, Marcus recognized the need for sensitivity in their interactions. Matseleng's trauma had an uncanny ability to resurface unexpectedly, casting a shadow over their moments of joy and connection.

On a particular morning, Marcus wore a new perfume he had recently acquired. Unbeknownst to him, its aroma bore a striking resemblance to the fragrance her uncle used to wear. Upon returning home from work, he found Matseleng in a moody state which he couldn't fathom. Throughout the day, she had expressed feelings of emotional turmoil. Eager to offer comfort, Marcus sought to embrace her, only to be met with her pushing him away and a scream of distress.

The scent of the perfume was a trigger, subconsciously evoking memories tied to her abuser. Although the fragrance wasn't overpowering, its presence in the house had rekindled recollections of her painful past. At that moment, Matseleng was overwhelmed, unable to speak. The scent that lingered on Marcus made her feel as though she were in the grasp of her abuser's hold.

Vivid memories resurfaced, reminding her of the dark times she had endured while living under the same roof as him. The scent had become synonymous with the countless nights of violation she had experienced, his presence in her room marked by silence and unwelcome touch.

During this episode, she found herself unable to allow Marcus's touch, seeking refuge at the edge of the bed. Marcus's bewilderment deepened until Matseleng finally found the strength to share her anguish. Promptly, he removed the perfume from their lives, and their routine began to restore itself.

Marcus recognized the depth of Matseleng's feelings and was determined not to jeopardize her healing process. He understood the delicate balance of allowing vulnerability in their relationship while guarding against unintentional triggers. Although their love was young, he was committed to providing the unwavering support and understanding Matseleng required.

Looking into her eyes made her feel vulnerable, but it was a different kind of vulnerability that was not connected to her trauma. Matseleng was an introvert, and part of that was because of her trauma. She started distancing herself from other kids after that incident. She had always thought that she was the only person who understood herself, but whenever Marcus looked into her eyes, he would say things that made her feel like he knew her far much more than she could bear.

"Did I trigger you?" he inquired.

"Of course not, what makes you think you have?" she asked with curiosity.

"The shivers on your spine?" he responded.

The Art Of Making Love

At this moment, Matseleng knew how fortunate she was to be engaged to a kind and considerate man. She even pinched herself to check if she was not dreaming. His sensitivity to her emotional well-being was overwhelming. She shed a tear as she thought deeply about it.

There was a time in her life when she thought that all men are the same, but here she is, she has met a man who is different. Matseleng knew that her life was in safe hands and she cherished every moment they shared. This made her feel even safer with Marcus because she now understood how much he cared for her well-being.

"Now you are sending more shivers down my spine because you are too good to be true. Are you sure you are not a ghost?" She said in an emotional tone.

Marcus breathed a sigh of relief; he felt that he was on the right track, and her words warmed his heart. All he wanted was to create a safe environment for her. He felt that life had thrown rocks at her for the longest time, and that it was his responsibility to fix that.

He wanted to be her knight in shining armor, and her text had just confirmed that he is not so far from his dream.

"I had never thought I would be engaged to such a considerate and loving man. I have never seen myself deserving that, and I always saw myself as dirty and unworthy of good men like yourself; I feel honored," she texted back while he was still excited from her previous text.

Marcus knew just how to love her in places where she felt most vulnerable. He worshipped her and gave her treatment worthy of a queen. He did not want her to be bruised, and this became his obsession.

Lessons learned:

In the dynamic between Marcus and Matseleng, we find a profound exploration of vulnerability and the healing power of love. Their journey teaches us valuable lessons about how partners can support each other through past traumas and scars, creating a deep sense of emotional intimacy and understanding.

Matseleng's past trauma, stemming from childhood sexual abuse, left her with deep-seated fears and triggers that sometimes manifested in their intimate moments. Her vulnerability in these instances reflects the lingering wounds she carries and the need for a supportive and understanding partner like Marcus.

Marcus's initial struggle to comprehend Matseleng's reactions highlights the importance of open communication and empathy in navigating past traumas within a relationship. Over time, they engage in heartfelt conversations that deepen their understanding of each other's pain and vulnerabilities.

The episode with the perfume serves as an example of how unintentional triggers can evoke painful memories and disrupt emotional intimacy. Marcus's swift action to remove the perfume from their lives demonstrates his commitment to Matseleng's healing and well-being, prioritizing her comfort and emotional safety above all else.

Through Marcus's sensitivity and unwavering support, Matseleng experiences a profound shift in her perception of love and relationships. She discovers that not all men are the same, finding solace and security in Marcus's kindness and consideration. Their bond grows stronger as Matseleng realizes the depth of Marcus's care for her well-being, creating a deep sense of trust and gratitude within their relationship.

In moments of vulnerability, Marcus's ability to see and understand Matseleng on a soul-deep level brings her comfort and reassurance. His genuine concern for her emotional well-being leaves Matseleng feeling cherished and valued, reinforcing the strength of their connection and deepening their intimacy.

Ultimately, their journey underscores the transformative power of love in healing past wounds and building emotional intimacy. By embracing vulnerability and offering unconditional support, partners can create a safe and nurturing space where healing can flourish, paving the way for a deeply fulfilling and resilient relationship.

The soul-full orgasmic experience transcends the emotional and physical realms, catapulting the relationship into deeper dimensions of intimacy and connection. It is a profound union of souls that goes beyond mere emotional or physical satisfaction, touching the deepest parts of each partner's being and igniting a transformative journey of love and self-discovery.

Unlike the emotional orgasmic experience, which arises from deep emotional connection and vulnerability, the soul-full orgasmic experience delves into the essence of who we are as individuals and as partners. It occurs when two souls merge in a moment of profound intimacy, creating a sense of oneness and unity that surpasses the boundaries of time and space.

This soul-full orgasmic experience is characterized by a profound sense of spiritual ecstasy and fulfillment. It is a moment of divine connection where partners feel deeply aligned with each other, experiencing a sense of bliss and harmony that transcends earthly constraints.

As partners surrender to this soul-full orgasmic experience, they tap into the infinite reservoir of love and compassion that resides within them. It is a sacred union of hearts and souls, where love flows freely and unconditionally, nurturing and nourishing the relationship at its core.

This deepening of intimacy and connection through the soul-full orgasmic experience can lead to profound transformation within the relationship. It opens the door to deeper levels of trust, vulnerability, and understanding, allowing partners to explore new dimensions of themselves and each other.

Moreover, the soul-full orgasmic experience has the power to heal past wounds and traumas, offering a sense of wholeness and completeness that transcends earthly limitations. It is a journey of self-discovery and self-acceptance, where partners come to fully embrace and celebrate their true essence.

In essence, the soul-full orgasmic experience is a sacred union of hearts and souls that elevates the relationship to higher realms of love and consciousness. It is a reminder of the infinite potential that lies within each of us to experience profound love, joy, and connection, and a testament to the transformative power of love in all its forms.

The Story Of Marcus and Matseleng: Building Anticipation

15:06

The yearning for the evening grew deeper as the day progressed; every minute that went by felt like forever. Marcus, a journalist at a prominent Media House, could not escape his daily duty to be with his queen. He was working on a project that was due that afternoon, and he had no choice but to work on completing it before he left the office.

Not that their emotionally charged and intimate chats were helping; he would often get caught up in a cloud and start imagining himself in a very compromising position with Matseleng. He could not wait to have his skin make contact with hers. The thought of it sent shock waves throughout his body, and he would just freeze in a moment while thinking of her.

"Right now you are interfering with my progress, babes. I can't seem to focus anymore..." he texted.

Matseleng burst into laughter, excited to notice that she had him all to herself.

"I love you, and you are the most important thing that matters to me. What you have been through as a child does not change the way I see you. To me, you are a whole new being, the old has passed, and it is the here and now I will forever cherish," he texted back while she was caught up in an emotional rollercoaster.

She was now sitting on the bed, soaked in Marcus's flattery. She had plans to go to the market, but she procrastinated on account of their wholesome conversation. Marcus's words made her even more vulnerable, and she was willing to be his slave, and him, her master. She had never felt so safe in a man's arms, and sometimes it was even scary.

"Your attempts to enslave me to your love are working like magic, Mister," she texted.

"My apologies, my lady, the plan is not to enslave you," he responded.

"Too late, you better come home already. Your slave is itching with the desire to serve you," she responded.

"I am the one who is a slave to this job I am doing. Why am I not with you right now?" he responded.

"Maybe you should just risk it and escape to your slave. Why be a slave there when you can be the master here?" she responded playfully.

"Do not put ideas in my head, My Queen..." he warned.

"Your slave, you meant?" She sought to correct him.

"I would rather be your slave and submit to your enchantments than be a queen in a castle elsewhere," she added.

At this time, Marcus was completely distracted from work, and he was making very little progress. He was caught up in a cloud he could hardly get in touch with his work.

There was a knock at his door, and it was his boss checking on the progress, which Marcus did not have much to show. Mr. Malose reiterated that the article should be ready for press release by 17:00 and he was not going to accept any excuses.

"My boss almost caught me texting. You might get me fired..." he reported to her.

She responded with gestures of shame and embarrassment, yet in a playful manner. They were both enjoying this moment, and the passion grew as they continued to text.

"You started this, My Lord..." she absolved herself from the guilt.

15:45

Marcus was an ink alchemist of exceptional skill. Mr. Malosi trusted him with the most complex projects, and he never disappointed. At this moment, he had to compile a report on a prominent politician, Mr. Mabaso, who was embroiled in a scandal related to tender allocation.

The story had been brewing, fueled by speculation. Now, new information had surfaced, causing every media house to scramble in a race to report on the latest developments.

Marcus knew he couldn't afford to be a minute later than he should be at the office, so he started working his magic. He swiftly gathered information from reliable sources and double-checked his facts.

"Why do I feel like I am being deprived of the attention I was getting?" she protested.

"Suspense is good; I'm sure you've been staring at your screen, anticipating my text," he playfully excused himself.

She rolled her eyes in disbelief but smiled.

The Art Of Making Love

"You got me there," she texted.

He chuckled.

"Your slave does not like to be kept waiting, My Lord..." she responded.

"...she turns into a desperate slave, begging for her Master's caresses," she continued.

"That doesn't sound bad at all..." he responded.

"I knew you would like that," she smiled as she texted.

Lessons Learned:

The passage from the story of Marcus and Matseleng beautifully illustrates the art of building anticipation within a relationship, even when partners are temporarily apart due to work commitments. Through their playful and affectionate exchange of messages, Marcus and Matseleng create a sense of excitement and longing that heightens their anticipation for each other's presence.

One key aspect of building anticipation is the notion that "absence makes the heart grow fonder." Despite being physically separated by Marcus's work obligations, their yearning for each other grows stronger with every passing minute, fueling their desire to be reunited and share intimate moments together.

The exchange of playful banter and affectionate gestures deepens their emotional bond and intensifies their longing for each other. Marcus's playful excuses for his distraction at work and Matseleng's playful responses add an element of excitement and intrigue to their interaction, further heightening the anticipation for their reunion.

Their willingness to express vulnerability and affection for each other also deepens their emotional intimacy and strengthens their bond.

Matseleng's willingness to be vulnerable with Marcus, despite her past traumas, speaks to the trust and comfort they share in their relationship.

Ultimately, the art of building anticipation lies in the ability to keep the spark of love alive, even in the midst of daily responsibilities and obligations. Marcus and Matseleng demonstrate that anticipation can be cultivated through playful exchanges and heartfelt messages, sustaining their love and keeping their relationship thriving, regardless of the temporary separation caused by work commitments.

The Story Of Marcus And Matseleng: Home At Last

17:05

Marcus finally makes his exit from the office, but now he has to face the traffic

17:30

As the sun began its slow descent, casting a warm golden hue across the city, Marcus navigated the familiar route home. His thoughts were split between the traffic and the anticipation of reuniting with Matseleng.

Meanwhile, Matseleng was busy in their kitchen, orchestrating her culinary symphony. The aroma of spices and sizzling ingredients filled the air, an evidence to her prowess as a kitchen art master. She was wearing Marcus' white shirt which exposed her butt cheeks; she moved gracefully between countertops, her mind wandering as she thought of Marcus.

"How's the traffic treating you, My Lord?" She disrupted the silence.

Marcus glanced at his phone, a smile tugging at his lips. With a quick glance at the road, he typed his response.

"It's the usual chaos, but I can't complain when I have you waiting for me," he explained.

"Well, don't keep me waiting too long. I have a surprise for you tonight," she teased.

Marcus's curiosity was piqued. He tapped his fingers on the steering wheel, his anticipation growing.

"A surprise? Now you've really got my attention. What's the occasion?" He curiously enquired.

"You are the occasion, My Lord, just my way of reminding you how much you mean to me," she texted.

The traffic moved at a snail's pace, but Marcus hardly noticed. Matseleng's words warmed his heart, and he imagined her smiling as she sent those messages.

"You always know how to make me feel special, even from a distance," he said as he became emotional.

"Wait till you see what I've cooked up. It might just distract you from the traffic," she kept teasing him.

Marcus chuckled, imagining Matseleng's mischievous grin. The messages became a lifeline, connecting them despite the physical distance.

"You've got me intrigued now. I can't wait to be home," he responded with anticipation.

"Just a little while longer, my love. Drive safely," she said.

The traffic eased slightly, allowing Marcus to relax his grip on the steering wheel. The sun's glow had turned into a warm embrace, mirroring the warmth he felt from their conversation.

18:15

The Art Of Making Love

Finally, Marcus turned into Dinoko Avenue, his heart racing with anticipation. As he parked the car, he caught a glimpse of Matseleng through the window, her silhouette moving gracefully in the kitchen.

He stepped out of the car and walked toward their front door, a sense of belonging enveloped him. He was about to step into a world where his skills as an ink alchemist were embraced, and his love for Matseleng was celebrated.

Matseleng was a beautiful woman with dark skin and thick thighs. She wore his white shirt, which was obviously not long enough to cover her butt cheeks. She stood barefoot by the kitchen counter, holding a bottle of wine and two glasses.

Marcus stood there, amazed by her alluring appearance. He looked at her as if it were the first time he had laid eyes on her. He gazed at her with desire, drawn to her cleavage that resembled twin mountains, a landscape that ignited a deeper longing for her.

"I told you I would be barely dressed," she broke the silence.

Without many words, Matseleng walked towards him and embraced him. Despite her shorter stature, she stood on her toes as they kissed passionately. Their yearning for each other deepened, and they were on the verge of surrendering to their desires. He began caressing her thick thighs as their lips met. As he reached her sizable buttocks, he realized she wasn't wearing underwear.

"You're not wearing underwear," he whispered.

"It's not like I didn't warn you," she responded with a whisper.

"You're so wet," he noted.

"I blame your texts," she defended herself.

He started unbuttoning the shirt she was wearing, and discarded his T-shirt, letting it fall to the kitchen floor. She untied his belt and unzipped his trousers. She slid her hand inside his trousers, and she touched his already hardened shaft.

Kneeling down, she pulled his trousers down to get an unobstructed view of his rigid arousal.

"My Master's magic wand," she said in a seductive tone.

She sensually caressed it with her hands, her lips making contact with the tip of his penis while her other hand softly stroked his scrotum. Marcus held onto her head as if his life depended on it. With gentle and consistent movements, she sucked on the tip of his penis until Marcus teetered on the brink of orgasmic rapture, before releasing her 'prisoner'.

"I'm going to serve you as your slave, My Lord," she whispered seductively. She lightly kissed the base of his erect member before taking it into her mouth. His moans grew as she skillfully moved her lips and tongue along his length. Her determination to please him knew no bounds.

As she continued, Marcus's moans became more intense. He was completely lost in the moment, consumed by pleasure, and at the heart of his desire.

He reached out to her, lifting her from the floor and placing her on the kitchen counter.

"May I return the favor, My Lady?" he asked.

Without waiting for her answer, he parted her legs and positioned her at the edge of the counter. He began with soft kisses on her thighs, alternating between left and right before venturing further. He explored her delicate anatomy, gently caressing her clitoris with his lips and occasionally using his tongue. He maintained a steady pace as he wanted to ensure that she reached certain levels of her orgasmic experience. Marcus was a patient man, and he was never in a hurry when he was down there. At this moment, he made her the point of focus, and her pleasure was his priority. The longer he focused his attention on her clitoris, the more her pleasurable moans increased and her grip on him tightened.

"I'm coming," she exclaimed in ecstasy.

Maintaining the same rhythm, he guided her to new heights of pleasure, eliciting her first orgasm. He stood by, sustaining the pace to allow her to fully experience her orgasmic energy. She trembled atop the kitchen counter, and Marcus savored witnessing her ascend to such heights of ecstasy. Then, lifting his head, he planted kisses on her belly button, slowly trailing upward with tender kisses until he reached her erect nipples, which he caressed with gentle strokes.

She eagerly grasped his shaft as Marcus drew nearer. Her desire had peaked, and she trembled with anticipation. All she yearned for now was for Marcus to be inside her. Matseleng surrendered completely to desire, giving herself to Marcus in a way she never had with anyone else. She pulled him towards her, guiding his shaft inside her.

With a gentle thrust, he slowly entered her, honoring her unspoken plea. Marcus entered her depths, and for a moment, they both basked in the overwhelming pleasure. He withdrew briefly, leaving her feeling a pang of loss, but at her silent request, he returned. It was a moment that seemed to stretch on forever, the experience surreal.

As he continued his rhythmic thrusts, their pleasure intensified, and they moaned deeply, savoring each moment. This was the culmination of their desires, a moment where they lost all control to the waves of pleasure crashing over them. At the peak of their ecstasy, they both experienced intense orgasms, their passionate cries echoing through the hallways of their humble home.

The Art Of Making Love

As their breaths finally steadied, Matseleng and Marcus held each other close, their bodies still entwined in the aftermath of their passionate encounter. The air was thick with a mix of contentment and desire, a tangible reminder of the deep connection they shared.

Matseleng's fingers traced lazy circles on Marcus's chest as they basked in the afterglow.

With a gentle smile, she whispered, "You know, I never thought I'd find someone who could make me feel safe and cherished like you do."

Marcus met her gaze with tenderness in his eyes. "And I never imagined I'd find someone who could awaken such a fierce need within me, yet also calm the storms that have always raged within."

They remained wrapped in each other's arms, the world outside their intimate bubble fading into insignificance. The day's buildup of desire and anticipation had been released in a crescendo of pleasure, leaving them both feeling more connected than ever before.

They exchanged whispered words and shared soft kisses, weaving promises of love and devotion into their intimate moment. They talked about their dreams, their fears, and the scars that had shaped them, each revelation bringing them closer

Eventually, exhaustion tugged at their senses, a reminder that the night was still young and they have not had their dinner yet. Matseleng and Marcus reluctantly disentangled themselves, Marcus poured two glasses of wine, while Matseleng prepared dinner.

Lessons Learned:

As Marcus finally leaves work and returns home to Matseleng, their reunion is left to the imagination, yet the anticipation and longing they've built throughout the day set the stage for a deeply fulfilling and intimate encounter. Their playful banter, affectionate messages, and shared vulnerability have laid the foundation for a connection that transcends the physical realm.

In reflecting on Marcus and Matseleng's journey, we are reminded of the importance of emotional intimacy in building up a strong and resilient relationship. Their willingness to open up to each other, express vulnerability, and offer unwavering support highlights the transformative power of emotional connection in deepening love and trust.

Moreover, their soul-full intimacy, characterized by a profound union of hearts and souls, elevates their relationship to higher realms of love and consciousness. Through moments of spiritual connection and shared understanding, they experience a sense of oneness and unity that transcends earthly constraints.

Building anticipation plays a pivotal role in sustaining the spark of love and keeping the flame of desire alive. Marcus and Matseleng's playful exchanges and longing for each other create a sense of excitement and longing that heightens their anticipation for each other's presence, enriching their connection and deepening their intimacy.

Ultimately, the height of sexual pleasure lies in the artful integration of emotional intimacy, soul-full connection, and anticipation. When these elements converge, the result is a profoundly pleasurable and transformative experience that transcends the physical act of intimacy. It is an orgasmic experience that encompasses the depths of the soul, the heights of emotional connection, and the exhilaration of anticipation, leaving couples feeling deeply fulfilled and connected on every level.

Marcus and Matseleng's journey serves as an evidence to the transformative power of love and intimacy. By nurturing emotional connection, creating soul-full intimacy, and building anticipation, couples can create a relationship that is truly fulfilling and deeply satisfying, both emotionally and sexually.

The Art Of Making Love

As Marcus finally arrives home, the anticipation and longing that have been building throughout the day reach a crescendo. Both he and Matseleng are primed and ready for the physical exploration of each other, having engaged in a subtle yet potent form of foreplay through their playful banter, affectionate messages, and shared vulnerability.

Throughout the day, Marcus and Matseleng have been preparing each other for this moment, teasing and tantalizing each other with their words and gestures. Their playful exchanges have sparked a fire of desire that now burns brightly, igniting their passion and fueling their longing to connect on a physical level.

Physiologically, their bodies are primed and ready for intimacy, with heightened arousal and increased sensitivity to touch. The anticipation and excitement they've cultivated throughout the day have activated their nervous systems, preparing them for the pleasurable sensations to come.

Yet, it is not just their bodies that are ready for this moment; their minds have also been cultivated for intercourse. Through their emotional intimacy and soul-full connection, Marcus and Matseleng have created a deep sense of trust and intimacy that allows them to fully surrender to each other's touch and embrace.

As they come together in this moment of physical intimacy, they do so with a profound sense of connection and mutual desire. Their bodies and minds align in a symphony of pleasure and ecstasy, as they explore each other with a sense of curiosity, passion, and love.

In this way, the physical exploration of each other becomes not just a culmination of their day-long anticipation, but a celebration of their deep emotional and spiritual connection. It is a moment of profound intimacy and joy, where they come together as one, united in their love and desire for each other.

Lessons From Their Sex Play

In the act of lovemaking, Marcus and Matseleng, having built up tension throughout the day, found themselves ready to deepen their connection through intercourse. Typically, it takes between 15 to 20 minutes of foreplay to prepare a woman for vaginal penetration. However, when foreplay has been ongoing, the mind and body are primed for intimacy. By the time Marcus arrived home, Matseleng was already in a state of readiness; a simple kiss was all it took to awaken her desire and prepare her physically.

The Power of Anticipation: Marcus and Matseleng's day was filled with anticipation, building the tension between them as they looked forward to their reunion. Anticipation can be a powerful tool in enhancing intimacy, as it heightens desire and creates a sense of longing for each other.

The Importance of Foreplay: Foreplay plays a crucial role in preparing both partners for intercourse. While it typically takes between 15 to 20 minutes of foreplay to prepare a woman for vaginal penetration, ongoing anticipation and stimulation throughout the day can significantly shorten this time frame. Matseleng's state of readiness upon Marcus's arrival demonstrates the power of prolonged foreplay in priming the mind and body for intimacy.

Psychological Foreplay: Another powerful form of foreplay is psychological stimulation. Throughout the day, Marcus and Matseleng engaged in playful banter and exchanged messages filled with desire, further heightening their anticipation and arousal. This psychological foreplay not only prepares the mind for intimacy but also strengthens the emotional connection between partners.

Mind-Body Connection: The mind and body are intricately connected when it comes to sexual arousal. Matseleng's readiness for intimacy was not just physical but also psychological, as her anticipation and desire for

Marcus had been building throughout the day. This highlights the importance of nurturing both emotional and physical intimacy in a relationship.

Communication and Connection: Throughout their interaction, Marcus and Matseleng communicated openly and affectionately, strengthening their emotional connection. From their playful teasing to their tender expressions of love, their communication served to deepen their bond and enhance their intimacy.

Savoring the Moment: Marcus and Matseleng fully embraced the moment, allowing themselves to be completely present with each other. They savored every touch, kiss, and sensation, immersing themselves in the pleasure of the experience. This serves as a reminder to cherish and appreciate each intimate moment shared with a partner.

Mutual Pleasure: Their lovemaking was characterized by a focus on mutual pleasure and satisfaction. Marcus's attentiveness to Matseleng's needs and desires, and Matseleng's reciprocation, demonstrated the importance of prioritizing each other's pleasure in sexual encounters.

The Afterglow: After their passionate encounter, Marcus and Matseleng basked in the afterglow of their love, feeling a deep sense of connection and contentment. This highlights the importance of intimacy beyond the physical act of sex, emphasizing the emotional closeness and intimacy that follow a shared experience of pleasure.

Overall, Marcus and Matseleng's story serves as a reminder of the profound impact that anticipation, communication, and mutual pleasure can have on intimacy and connection in a relationship. By nurturing these aspects of their relationship, couples can deepen their bond and create fulfilling and meaningful experiences of intimacy together.

The Story Of Marcus and Matseleng: When The Lights Grow Deem

The moans that echoed through the hallways of their humble home from the kitchen counter were just the beginning of a steamy night. As Marcus and Matseleng had anticipated, the night was indeed special, and Matseleng had prepared a feast fit for royalty. They didn't just indulge in the pleasure of each other's company; they also savored the delectable dishes crafted by Matseleng, a culinary artist in her own right.

After dinner, they lingered at the table, savoring the flavors of both the food and their love, their conversation punctuated by shared laughter and tender glances. Eventually, they moved to the cozy confines of their living room, where they settled into each other's arms, enveloped by the soft strains of music that filled the room.

They sat intertwined, relishing the warmth of each other's embrace and the gentle rhythm of their breathing. In this moment of quiet intimacy, they found solace and contentment, their hearts beating in harmony as they reveled in the simple joy of being together.

As the night unfolded, Marcus and Matseleng found themselves drawn to the bathroom, shedding their clothes along the way, eager to immerse themselves in the soothing embrace of warm water. Stepping into the shower, they were enveloped by the steamy tendrils, the sensation adding to the already charged atmosphere between them. Beneath the cascading spray, they stood close, their bodies pressed together in a sensual embrace, their skin tingling with anticipation.

In the intimate confines of the shower, they embarked on a journey of a steamy exploration, their hands tracing each other's curves and contours with gentle caresses and lingering kisses. Marcus's lips roamed over Matseleng's skin, leaving a trail of soft kisses in their wake, each touch igniting a fire of desire within them.

Their desire for each other intensified with each passing moment, driving them to patiently and thoroughly explore every inch of each other's bodies. Marcus's hands roamed freely, tracing the curves of Matseleng's form with deliberate precision, committing every contour to memory. Meanwhile, Matseleng luxuriated in the sensation of Marcus's touch, each caress sending electric waves of pleasure coursing through her body.

Understanding Foreplay

Foreplay is not just about stimulating arousal; it is a deeply intimate and exploratory journey where partners embrace and celebrate each other's bodies, emotions, and desires.

Physically, foreplay involves sensual and affectionate activities such as kissing, caressing, and touching erogenous zones. These actions serve to awaken the senses, heighten arousal, and prepare the body for sexual activity. However, beyond mere physical stimulation, foreplay is a profound exploration of each other's bodies. It is a time to appreciate the unique curves, textures, and sensations that make each partner unique. Through gentle touch and exploration, partners learn about each other's preferences, sensitivities, and pleasure points, deepening their understanding and connection.

Moreover, foreplay is an emotional play, a dance of intimacy and vulnerability that strengthens the emotional bond between partners. It involves verbal and non-verbal communication, where partners express their desires, fantasies, and affection for each other. Through whispered words, longing glances, and tender gestures, partners convey their love and desire, creating a safe and intimate space for sexual exploration. Emotional foreplay builds trust, openness, and vulnerability, allowing partners to deepen their connection and intimacy.

It's crucial for couples to understand the importance of taking their time during foreplay, without rushing towards penetration. Foreplay is not just a prelude to sex; it's an integral part of the sexual experience that sets the stage for deeper intimacy and pleasure. Rushing through foreplay can diminish the overall satisfaction and connection between partners.

One common mistake many men make during foreplay is being too quick to focus solely on the genitals. This approach can be uncomfortable, especially if the genitals are not yet ready for direct touch. Instead, it's essential to explore various pleasure spots throughout the body before moving to the genitals. By taking the time to explore these areas, arousal can build gradually, and the genitals will naturally become more receptive to touch.

As you explore your partner's pleasure spots, her body will respond by lubricating, making it easier and more enjoyable to touch and explore her genitals. This gradual progression allows for a more pleasurable and satisfying sexual experience for both partners, creating deeper intimacy and connection.

Moreover, a woman can sense when a man is in a hurry for penetration during foreplay, and this might cause an uneasy feeling, killing the vibe for the entire session. As we have already alluded to, foreplay is an emotional play. It is important to understand that how you make her feel emotionally at this stage is critically important and could determine the direction you are taking. The last thing you want to do is to provoke her anxiety levels, which are often barriers to reaching an orgasm.

So, when you are down there, send through a message to her that you are not in a hurry and you are there to stay. This will relax her and make her feel more emotionally connected to your nonverbal cues. In this way, her focus will be on the pleasure and will most definitely take her into a world of her own.

It's also important to acknowledge that women's genitals typically take longer to become fully aroused and ready for sexual activity compared to men. The process of arousal for women involves increased blood flow to the genital area, which takes time to reach its peak. Therefore, it's essential for the man to take his time to explore and stimulate his partner's pleasure spots, allowing her arousal to build gradually.

Research suggests that it can take around 10 minutes or more of focused stimulation to fully arouse a woman. During this time, it's crucial for the man to be patient, attentive, and responsive to his partner's cues and feedback.

By taking the time to enjoy each other's bodies and sensations, couples can create a pathway to deeper intimacy and pleasure. Engaging in extended foreplay not only enhances physical arousal but also creates emotional connection and intimacy between partners. It's an opportunity to communicate desires, explore fantasies, and build anticipation for the sexual experience ahead.

So, prioritizing extended foreplay allows couples to fully engage in the pleasures of touch, exploration, and intimacy. By taking their time and being attuned to each other's needs, couples can enhance their sexual satisfaction, deepen their emotional connection, and create a more fulfilling and pleasurable sexual experience.

Foreplay is a celebration of love, desire, and intimacy between partners. It is a time to revel in the beauty of each other's bodies, minds, and souls, and to nurture the deep emotional connection that lies at the heart of their relationship. By embracing the exploration of each other's bodies and emotions, partners can deepen their bond, enhance their sexual satisfaction, and experience profound intimacy and connection in their relationship.

Oral Sex is Sex

Oral sex is a vital aspect of sexual intimacy and should be recognized as such. Research indeed indicates that a significant percentage of women do not achieve orgasm through penile penetration alone. For many women, clitoral stimulation is essential for reaching orgasm, and oral sex can be an incredibly effective way to provide this stimulation.

In fact, studies have shown that the clitoris, which contains thousands of nerve endings, is the primary source of sexual pleasure for most women. Therefore, understanding a woman's sexual anatomy, including the structure and function of the clitoris, is crucial for providing her with maximum pleasure.

Moreover, it's essential to recognize that oral sex is not just an alternative to penetration; it's a legitimate and fulfilling form of sexual activity in its own right. By focusing on oral sex, partners can explore new sensations, enhance arousal, and deepen intimacy.

For men, excelling in oral sex requires more than just knowing a woman's pleasure spots; it involves understanding her unique anatomy and preferences. This includes knowing how to stimulate the clitoris effectively, as well as being attentive to her responses and cues. Communication is key; partners should feel comfortable discussing their desires, boundaries, and preferences openly.

Furthermore, men should approach oral sex with a mindset of pleasure-giving rather than performance. It's not about achieving a specific goal or proving one's prowess; it's about connecting with your partner on a deeper level and prioritizing her pleasure and satisfaction.

It's important to recognize that the most sensual sexual organs of a woman, critical to giving her an orgasm, are not internal but external. The clitoris, often referred to as the "seat of female pleasure," is the primary source of sexual stimulation and orgasm for many women. Despite its small size, the clitoris contains thousands of nerve endings, making it highly sensitive to touch and capable of producing intense sensations of pleasure.

Unlike the penis, which is primarily external but also contains the urethra and other structures within the body, the clitoris is external. This means that direct stimulation of the clitoris, whether through manual touch, oral sex, or other forms of stimulation, is essential for many women to achieve orgasm.

In addition to the clitoris, other external erogenous zones such as the labia, perineum, and breasts can also contribute to a woman's sexual pleasure and arousal. By exploring and stimulating these areas, partners can enhance arousal, build anticipation, and deepen intimacy during sexual activity.

Understanding the importance of external sexual organs in female pleasure highlights the need for partners to prioritize clitoral stimulation and other external erogenous zones during sexual encounters. By focusing on these areas and being attentive to a woman's responses and cues, partners can increase the likelihood of mutual satisfaction and pleasure.

Ultimately, recognizing and celebrating the significance of external sexual organs in female pleasure underscores the importance of communication, exploration, and mutual pleasure in sexual relationships. By embracing the full spectrum of female sexuality and pleasure, partners can create more fulfilling and satisfying sexual experiences together.

Just as women have pleasure spots that are critical to their sexual pleasure, men also have erogenous zones that can contribute to their enjoyment and satisfaction during sexual activity. While vaginal penetration can be pleasurable for men, it's essential to recognize that it's not the only pathway to maximum sexual pleasure.

Men have a variety of erogenous zones, including the penis, scrotum, perineum, and nipples, which can all contribute to their sexual arousal and pleasure. For many men, receiving oral sex can be an incredibly pleasurable experience that enhances arousal, builds anticipation, and deepens intimacy with their partner.

The penis, in particular, is highly sensitive to touch and stimulation, making it a focal point for sexual pleasure. Oral sex, with its direct and intimate contact, can provide intense sensations of pleasure and arousal for men, leading to powerful orgasms and a heightened sense of satisfaction.

In addition to the penis, other erogenous zones such as the scrotum, perineum (the area between the anus and the scrotum), and nipples can also be sources of pleasure for men. By exploring and stimulating these areas, partners can enhance arousal, increase sensitivity, and create more fulfilling sexual experiences.

Recognizing that men too have pleasure spots underscores the importance of mutual pleasure and satisfaction in sexual relationships. Just as partners prioritize clitoral stimulation and other external erogenous zones for women, they should also be attentive to men's needs and desires during sexual activity.

By embracing the full spectrum of pleasure and exploring each other's bodies with curiosity and enthusiasm, partners can create a more intimate, fulfilling, and satisfying sexual connection. Ultimately, prioritizing mutual pleasure and communication allows couples to deepen their bond and create lasting sexual satisfaction and fulfillment together.

Lubrication

It's important to acknowledge that sometimes, for best results and enhanced pleasure, the use of lubricants is advised during sexual activity. Lubricants can reduce friction, increase comfort, and enhance sensations, making sexual experiences more enjoyable and satisfying for both partners.

When the genitals are not adequately lubricated, whether due to natural lubrication or arousal, friction can occur during sexual activity, leading to discomfort or even pain. This can be particularly true for activities such as penetration or prolonged oral sex.

For women, in particular, insufficient lubrication can be a common issue, especially during certain times in their menstrual cycle, menopause, or when taking certain medications. Using a water-based or silicone-based lubricant can help alleviate dryness, enhance comfort, and increase pleasure during sexual activity.

Moreover, both the penis and the female genital organs can be touch-sensitive when they are dry. Without sufficient lubrication, friction can lead to irritation, discomfort, and even minor injuries to the delicate tissues of the genitals. This can detract from the overall enjoyment and satisfaction of sexual activity.

By using lubricants, couples can ensure a smoother, more pleasurable sexual experience, allowing for increased comfort, sensitivity, and enjoyment for both partners. Additionally, lubricants can be incorporated into foreplay, enhancing sensations and increasing arousal, leading to more fulfilling and satisfying sexual encounters.

Ultimately, the use of lubricants can enhance intimacy, pleasure, and satisfaction during sexual activity, promoting a deeper connection and mutual enjoyment between partners. By prioritizing comfort and sensitivity, couples can create more enjoyable and fulfilling sexual experiences together.

The Story of Marcus and Matseleng: The Dance

...as they became increasingly lost in the intoxicating pleasure of their connection, they surrendered to the moment, allowing their passion and ecstasy to reach new heights with every passing second. Marcus, overcome by desire, gently turned Matseleng around and pressed her

against the sleek surface of the shower glass, her breasts pressed sensuously against the cool pane as he entered her from behind.

Despite the muffled sounds of their passion, partially obscured by the rush of water from the shower, their moans of pleasure echoed in the confined space, a symphony of desire that reverberated off the tiled walls. In that moment, they were consumed by the raw intensity of their connection, their bodies moving in perfect harmony as they danced to the rhythm of their shared desire.

After the thrill of thunderous orgasms, they stood together, basking in the gentle cascade of water from the shower in sheer silence. It was a moment of profound intimacy, where words were rendered unnecessary as they communicated their love and satisfaction through the unspoken language of touch and presence. Only the soothing sound of water filled the confined space, enveloping them in a cocoon of tranquility...

Beyond Foreplay

As you transition from foreplay to penetration, it's important to recognize the significance of this moment. The culmination of foreplay sets the stage for penetration, making it a deeply intimate and potentially transformative experience. The emotional and soulful connection that has been cultivated during foreplay enhances the intensity and meaning of penetration.

Penetration can be a profound expression of love and vulnerability between partners, but it's crucial to approach it with care and understanding. The quality of the moment depends on how it is approached and executed. It's important to remember that penetration is not just a physical act; it's an emotional and spiritual exchange as well.

At the moment of penetration, she may have already experienced multiple orgasms during foreplay. While she may still be capable of experiencing orgasm through penetration, allowing you to penetrate her is her way of expressing love and trust. It's a gesture that goes beyond physical pleasure and speaks to the depth of her emotional connection with you.

This is a moment of profound intimacy where the exchange of body fluids symbolizes a deeper merging of souls. By allowing herself to be vulnerable to you, she is spiritually and emotionally becoming one with you. In her mind, she embraces both your angels and demons, feeling a sense of unity and belonging.

When foreplay is done correctly, her primary focus may not be on achieving orgasm during penetration. Instead, she derives satisfaction from giving you pleasure and fulfilling her mental and emotional needs. It's about creating a space of mutual trust, pleasure, and fulfillment, where both partners can experience a profound connection and intimacy.

The element of trust plays a crucial role during the phase of intimacy that involves penetration. When a man penetrates a woman, various possibilities and consequences come into play, highlighting the importance of trust in the relationship.

Firstly, there's the possibility of pregnancy or the transmission of sexually transmitted infections (STIs). Whether she is not ready for pregnancy or is actively trying to conceive, allowing penetration involves a degree of risk and vulnerability. By engaging in intercourse, she entrusts her reproductive health and future to her partner, emphasizing the significance of trust in their relationship.

Moreover, penetration goes beyond physicality; it delves into the realm of emotions and vulnerability. For many women, sex is deeply emotional, and allowing someone to penetrate them signifies a high level of emotional trust. By opening herself up in such a manner, she exposes her innermost thoughts, desires, and vulnerabilities to her partner, laying bare her emotional landscape.

It's important to recognize that the act of penetration involves mutual trust and vulnerability for both partners, regardless of gender. While the risks and vulnerabilities may differ between men and women, both individuals are entrusting themselves to each other in deeply significant ways.

For men, the physical aspect of penetration may indeed be more pronounced in terms of pleasure and satisfaction, as it often marks the culmination of sexual arousal and desire. However, there's also an emotional component at play that should not be overlooked. As a man penetrates his partner, he exposes himself not only to physical risks but also to emotional vulnerability.

In this intimate moment, he opens himself up to his partner's emotional persona, allowing her into his innermost thoughts, desires, and vulnerabilities. He sees her as his peace and place of refuge, seeking comfort and connection in her presence. Despite the societal expectation that men prioritize physical pleasure over emotional intimacy, the act of penetration can hold deep emotional significance for them as well.

Moreover, men often experience emotional turmoil surrounding the responsibility of pregnancy, which can be left unattended and overlooked. This complex emotional state can cause chaos in relationships when a woman falls pregnant. Men's emotional investment in sexual intimacy communicates far more than just physical pleasure; it reflects a deep connection and emotional investment in their partner and the potential future they may share together.

Moreover, unlike women who may experience multiple orgasms, men typically have a single orgasm followed by a refractory period. Therefore, the moment of penetration often represents the pinnacle of pleasure and satisfaction for men. It's a time when they can fully immerse themselves in the physical sensations and emotional connection with their partner, experiencing a profound sense of fulfillment and intimacy.

Again I say, Communicate!

During this intimate and vulnerable time, communication becomes paramount. Just as it was crucial during foreplay, effective communication during penetration ensures that both partners are not only physically comfortable but also emotionally connected throughout the experience. Penetration, while often pleasurable, can also bring about discomfort or even pain, particularly for women. Moreover, certain positions may pose challenges to men, especially when the woman takes the lead. By openly communicating preferences, concerns, and boundaries, partners can navigate these potential obstacles together, creating a deeper sense of trust and intimacy.

Furthermore, the moment of penetration serves as a profound opportunity to demonstrate care and consideration for your partner's well-being. Given the sensitivity of genital areas, prioritizing comfort and ease is essential. This involves not only verbal communication but also attentiveness to nonverbal cues and signals of discomfort. Additionally, creating an environment that is conducive to relaxation and pleasure is key. This may include factors such as ensuring privacy, setting the mood with dim lighting or soothing music, and using lubrication to enhance comfort and reduce friction.

In addition to verbal and environmental considerations, personal hygiene plays a crucial role in ensuring a positive experience during penetration. Both partners should prioritize cleanliness and grooming, as this not only enhances physical comfort but also contributes to overall confidence and enjoyment. Taking the time to freshen up and maintain good hygiene practices demonstrates respect and consideration for your partner, setting the stage for a more pleasurable and intimate encounter.

The Aftercare

After the intense passion and connection of lovemaking, it's crucial not to overlook the importance of aftercare. This is the precious moment after sex when partners can bask in each other's embrace and reaffirm their love and connection. Instead of simply turning away and drifting off to sleep, it's essential to take the time to nurture and affirm each other.

Many people experience feelings of anxiety and insecurity after sex, wondering if their partner enjoyed the experience as much as they did. It's important to recognize that during intercourse, partners can only imagine how the other is feeling; they don't actually feel their partner's sensations. This can lead to doubts and uncertainties creeping in, which is why aftercare is so vital.

During this post-coital period, partners have the opportunity to quiet those doubts and concerns by expressing love and appreciation for each other. This is a time to use verbal and nonverbal cues to reassure one another of the deep connection and pleasure shared during the intimate act. It's a chance to affirm the love and passion that was just expressed physically, strengthening the bond between partners even further.

By engaging in aftercare, couples can deepen their emotional connection and intimacy, creating a safe and nurturing space for vulnerability and love to flourish. It's a beautiful way to honor the intimacy shared and ensure that both partners feel valued and cherished in the aftermath of lovemaking.

Indeed, the aftercare following lovemaking sets the tone for the days to come and profoundly impacts the trajectory of the relationship. The words exchanged and the gestures shared during this intimate time have the power to resonate deeply and influence the dynamics between partners.

By taking the time to affirm each other's love and connection, couples strengthen their bond and reinforce feelings of closeness and trust. The vulnerability and openness displayed during aftercare nurture a sense of security and emotional intimacy, laying a foundation for continued growth and mutual support in the relationship.

After a deeply satisfying encounter, the night holds a different energy for the couple. The levels of satisfaction and fulfillment are at their peak, and the shared experience creates a lasting sense of joy and contentment. As they drift off to sleep, wrapped in each other's arms, they carry with them the warmth and reassurance of their love, ready to face whatever the future may hold, knowing they have each other's unwavering support and affection.

The story of Marcus and Matseleng: The Aftercare

...after mustering the strength to move, they reached over to turn off the shower, the sound of water diminishing to a gentle trickle before ceasing altogether. As they reached for their towels, their movements seemed somewhat disjointed, as if they were aliens who had just arrived in an unfamiliar world. With quick, almost hurried motions, they dried themselves off, eager to reunite in each other's arms once more.

The lotion was applied hastily, their skin absorbing the moisturizing balm as they anticipated the warmth and closeness awaiting them. Finally, they found themselves nestled together between the sheets, limbs entwined as they sought solace and comfort in each other's embrace.

In that moment, the world outside faded away, leaving only the two of them, united in a world of their own creation, where nothing else mattered but the intense connection they shared.

As they basked in the afterglow of their passion, Marcus and Matseleng knew that they had experienced something truly extraordinary. It was more than just a physical encounter—it was a soulful union, a merging of hearts and minds that left them both forever changed.

"Today was really special," said Marcus, his voice filled with tenderness.

"I told you today will be special," Matseleng responded with a soft smile. "And you kept the promise," Marcus continued, his gaze fixed on her with adoration.

"How could I not fulfill the promise when the promise is with me looking deeply into my eyes and making me shy," Matseleng replied, resting her chin on his chest, feeling a warmth spread through her at his gaze.

"I love you, Matseleng," Marcus declared, his voice filled with emotion as he leaned in closer.

"And I love you, Marcus," she responded, her voice equally emotional, her heart overflowing with love.

"I have never felt so vulnerable like I did tonight," Marcus confessed, his tone sincere.

"How vulnerable?" Matseleng inquired, her curiosity piqued.

"The manner in which I felt sold out to you, and that I could do just anything for you," Marcus explained. "It made me feel like a slave doing the bidding of his master. I was completely captured in your charms."

Matseleng's heart swelled with love and gratitude as she listened to Marcus's words. She wrapped her arms around him, holding him close, cherishing the depth of their connection. In this moment of vulnerability and honesty, they found a deeper understanding of each other and a profound appreciation for the love they shared.

"Lie to me, Marcus, lie to me," Matseleng said jokingly, her eyes sparkling with playful mischief yet genuine affection.

"It's how you said it that got me," Marcus replied with a chuckle, his heart warmed by her laughter.

They shared a moment of pure joy, their laughter filling the room with warmth and light. After a brief pause, Matseleng spoke again, her voice soft and sincere. "You have cast a spell over me, Marcus. I am totally enraptured in your love. I have never experienced intimacy the way I do with you. You're like a genie of some sort."

The Art Of Making Love

"So, you resort to lying to me because I lied to you?" Marcus teased, his eyes twinkling with amusement.

"No, I'm being honest. You make me feel things nobody else has ever made me feel," Matseleng confessed, her gaze tender and sincere.

Marcus was momentarily speechless, his heart overflowing with love and gratitude. "It takes two to tango, I guess we just have the best connection. I enjoy the best experience with you too," he finally said, his voice filled with warmth and affection.

In that moment, Marcus and Matseleng knew that their love was something truly special—a bond that transcended words and brought them closer together with each passing moment. With laughter and love, they embraced the magic of their connection, cherishing every moment they shared together.

Feeling Matseleng press even closer to him, Marcus couldn't help but smile, his heart overflowing with love for this woman who had captured his soul. After a short moment of silence, he noticed the familiar sound of Matseleng's gentle snoring, a sound that never failed to bring a smile to his face.

Curious, Marcus tilted his head slightly to confirm that Matseleng had indeed fallen asleep, her breathing steady and peaceful. Chuckling softly to himself, Marcus leaned in and planted a tender kiss on her forehead, his love for her swelling within him.

With a contented sigh, Marcus wrapped his arms around Matseleng, holding her close as she slept soundly beside him. In that moment, surrounded by the warmth and comfort of their love, Marcus felt a profound sense of peace wash over him. With a smile on his face, he closed his eyes and joined Matseleng in the realm of dreams, knowing that he was exactly where he belonged.